Hitch Haikoo

Jerry Kelly

Hitch Haikoo

Jerry Kelly

PRESS

Gambier, Ohio

Copyright © 2025 Jerry Kelly
All rights reserved

Chapter *Young Kyle*
copyright © 2025 Kyle W. Henderson
All rights reserved

ISBN 978-1-880977-72-9
Library of Congress Control Number: 2025907310
Published May 2025, Gambier, Ohio USA

Book design by Jerry Kelly
Cover image by Tusumaru

Fragment of "On Vacation" by Robert Creeley

A hearty hug of gratitude to Pamela Hollie for her sharp eye and pencil – and kind blessings to all who helped these stories find their way home – the hitchers and ramblers, my rolling hosts, all the gracious road ghosts.

for Lori Kelly

*Love is the
only way home*

— *Paul Strauss*

9 — Roads and Rambles
Hobos to Hippies — 13
15 — Origins
To the Shore — 20
23 — Gone to Dogs
Deeper in the Well — 29
33 — Ever Wonder?
The Composer — 42
53 — The Fates
The Flying Car — 58
62 — Fuzzy's Index Finger
Young Kyle — 69
98 — Greek Gangster, Gay Savior
Stolen Feast — 115
119 — Gothenburg, Nebraska
Creeley — 126
133 — Oklahoma City Weed
Back to Bob — 136
139 — Paul's Hitch Home
White Mike — 142
159 — Lysergic Snowstorm
Key West & Halfway Back — 164
171 — The Blockade
A Hop and Skip to Iowa — 182
185 — Toward Heaven Above
Oh Well — 193
194 — Road Surfing Portugal
Closer to God and What Comes Next — 211
216 — Hitch Haikoo

Roads and Rambles

Hitchhiking opens landscapes of unhitched travel, unexpected adventure, and odd situations of all shapes and temperaments. Like the greatest sports, it has a rich literature. These stories reflect my own hitchhiking travels and those of others as we recollect them.

As a young boy on a humble, woodsy family vacation in western Connecticut, I received the gift of the ramble. A kid named Jeremy gave it to me — he was nine, I was eight years old. We'd meet up in the morning after breakfast.

Cabin breakfast had a refreshing ritual urgency, my role being to listen for the clink of the milkman, then fetch milk bottles from porch to table, being careful not to jostle the layer of cream at the top of each bottle. With a rare chance for non-homogenized milk, my parents carefully poured off the cream to add to their coffee before we kids splashed the rest onto our cereal.

Jeremy appears from the early shade and asks me, "Wanna go on a ramble?"

The ramble, as I learn, is an unstructured walk, a heading off into the day without a particular destination, with no idea where we're going but with a steady, languid energy that eventually gets us there. We just walk and find what we find — up the road, out in the woods, down along the lake shore, over that hill, or on the other side of the highway. On a good day, a snake or other wild creature makes an appearance. Better yet, a cave or tunnel we can explore, daring each other forward as young boys do. Our rambles resonate with the vital grace of freedom.

Growing up in a big busy family with little money, all my teenaged earnings stashed away to pay for college, hitchhiking was my free transportation to and from the beach as a young teen, then trips to and from college in upstate New York and Quebec, then in spare times taking rambling adventures toward somewhere. Hitchhiking was an outgrowth of the ramble. I always had a destination, but it was still all about a zeal for freedom and what I'd discover on the way.

I was not alone. The counterculture emerging in postwar America had, at its core, an expansive outward attitude amplifying earlier nineteenth- and twentieth century visions of America and its freedoms. A foundation book of my generation and counterculture, *On the Road,* gives us Jack Kerouac's traveling grace just as he had it, by bus and by thumb. John Steinbeck's *The Grapes of Wrath* opens with Tom Joad hitchhiking home from prison. Douglas Adams' *Hitchhiker's Guide to the Galaxy* sees interstellar hitchhiking as an eventuality. Kurt Vonnegut's Kilgore Trout hitchhikes cross-country in *Breakfast of Champions,* and Sissy Hankshaw's freakish big thumbs make her a hitchhiking legend in *Even Cowgirls Get the Blues.* Perhaps most endearingly, comic Tony Hawks relates his tale of becoming a national sensation after losing a drunken bet and having to hitchhike around Ireland with a refrigerator in his book, *Round Ireland With a Fridge.*

As related in Jon Krakauer's *Into the Wild,* Chris McCandless hitchhiked across the western U.S. in the early 1990s, before finding that school bus at road's end in Alaska.

But perhaps most crucially, it was the American actor Edwin Neal who gave us, in 1974, the lunatic killer hitchhiker in the original *Texas Chain Saw Massacre.* Fears thus inspired infect people, our thoughts and habits; we respond with reflexive avoidance and surfeit of caution.

Hitchhiking is more than just catching rides. It stands for someting larger: basic human kindness. The vast majority of my rides were provided by people doing a simple favor for a someone they didn't know. Being kind to the passing stranger. Other longtime hitchers report the same – you meet the nicest people most of the time.

With humanity now leaning hard the other way, toward mistrust and fear, it's useful to remember that in my lifetime this one artifact of community – sharing a ride – was a common acceptable norm, now all but completely disappeared. As if we've become so fearful of each other, we've not only stopped hitchhiking but now find it hard to believe that we ever did, and lived to tell the stories.

Hobos to Hippies

But we did.

Hitchhiking became both a practical matter and a lunge for freedom in the hippie years, carried forth by early counterculture signifiers choosing to live and work outside prevailing mainstreams (but riding their wheels). The Interstate highway system gave travelers of all stripes – among them writers, poets, music makers, image makers, filmmakers – a physical network by which to hitch rides, ride roads, and craft working lives out of sync with, but also central to, the midcentury modern American mix.

Poet Tom Clark offers this take, hard won after a life hitching in the U.S. and abroad:

"…I suppose [hitchhiking] now has a reputation only a cut or two above that of serial homicide. But there was a time when things were otherwise… From what I gauge to be the general reception nowadays, it appears "we" have not proven to be such great ambassadors of international blessing as we may have thought ourselves in those golden days of yore."

Poet Robert Creeley once noted that, in earlier years, his friend, poet Robert Duncan, never owned a car and often hitched to get anywhere.

Duncan was also a world-class typist, could finger a manual typewriter with incredible speed and endurance, much as Jack Kerouac could. Living in San Francisco, he typed student papers and graduate theses for local universities to fashion a modest income.

Duncan once hitches a ride with a young guy, soon to discover in conversation the guy is a grad student in Literature and has just submitted the final notes for his doctoral thesis, on Duncan's poetry!

With a quiet glee Duncan informs him, "I know, I'm typing it now."

Origins

The term goes back to the Depression area, first noted 1920-25 as an Americanism, *hitch + hike* as a single word. Defined as, to travel by standing on the side of the road to solicit rides from passing vehicles, from the drivers and occupants of said vehicles, often with some debate over whether or not to pick you up. It is the chocolate milk of human kindness to share a ride in such a way.

Hitchhiking became a common means of travel in the U.S. in Great Depression times. Most people had little money, much less an automobile. Many faced the prospect of traveling great distances, near-penniless, in search of work.

Hitching rides was given tacit acceptance by the federal government during the years when the Federal Transient Bureau dealt with large numbers of unemployed persons migrating to find work, money, and a stable life somewhere. Transients were promised a room and a hot meal at Bureau camps across the country if they could reach them. By rail and roadway thumb were common means.

A percieved "transient problem" took root in the popular mind during the late 1920s and throughout the Great Depression years, with news media of the day discovering that people like to read scary stories. Men and boys set out to find work and became unhitched from any community, strangers in all. Their sheer numbers made them an issue of concern in towns, villages, and rural regions along the way. Hungry men en route carry fear and need with them. Settled locals everywhere wrangled with what to do with all the itinerant passers-through, and generally sought ways to push them along, down the highway toward anywhere but here. Treated them, in effect, as bums. But it must be said that many Americans were truly kind strangers – they fed the road boys, bedded them in barns, sheds and spare bedrooms, and provided small human comforts to their journey.

The hobo figure is a migratory worker specifically – a homeless vagabond wandering in search of work, *ho*meward *bo*und with home an unknown destination mapped by hope.

In 1937, H. L. Mencken wrote in *The American Language:*

Tramps and hobos are commonly lumped together, but in their own sight they are sharply differentiated. A hobo or bo is simply a migratory laborer; he may take some longish holidays, but sooner or later he returns to work. A tramp never works if it can be avoided; he simply travels. Lower than either is the bum, who neither works nor travels, save when prodded into motion by a policeman's nightstick.

Seeking work – seeking a working life somewhere – pointed the hobo toward an idea of home, ways to make work and home living facts. Over the next horizon, or down the road another day or week or month, lay a possibility of home, of work to make home. Walking the shoulder of the highway with what your pockets or a satchel can hold (or that classic tied cloth bundle knotted to the end of a stick, a bindle) – putting yourself into the stream of traveling humanity is an act of faith, trust and courage, an occasion for danger and comedy, for connecting in ways neither digital nor virtual, except in the sense that the thumb is a digit that can point up and out toward futures uncertain, places unknown, people endlessly various. Moments of sudden discovery, satori in transit, as in poet Bob Creeley's sense of the "endless arrival."

Down the highway. Anywhere but here. By the late 1930s a general alarm spreads about roving men generally and hitchhikers in particular. It's a time of rapid growth for news media, local and national radio and newspapers coloring curious minds with lurid crime tales. The reading public, it turns out, has quite the appetite for that sort of thing. Bad news travels fast and scary news is lightning. Innocent drivers robbed, sometimes killed; innocent hitchhikers sexually assaulted. Souls lost on both sides of the equation.

Fourteen U.S. states outlaw hitchhiking by 1937, and by 1950 it's illegal to hitchhike in over half the United States. Regardless, hitchhiking sees a resurgence in American postwar counterculture, with many people putting out the thumb for short hops or longer ones. Enforcement varies by locale and is often lax – by the early 1970s, troopers in most states ignore hitchers on interstate on-ramps as long as they stay off the main highway roadsides. In the northeast, Jersey troopers are rumored to be brutal in random encounters with thumb-riders. Pennsylvania troopers likewise. But if you stand on a highway ramp and you have a hand-scrawled sign saying BUFFALO or DES MOINES they usually don't bother you.

I learned the rules of the road en route by thumbing to the beach as a kid, then to and from college in upstate New York and Montreal, then many elsewheres. Layered upon the spirit of the ramble, now with discovery and destination aligning, I realize an expansive freedom with a counterculture outlook that I seem, at some level, able to shape. I'm always lucky and get skilled at making my own luck.

And it began with rides to the beach.

To the Shore

The car is a black 1950 Plymouth Deluxe two-door fastback, my parents' first wheels. It's heavy and round, formed of real American steel, and feels just as fluidly solid as our new life in the new suburbs of New York City. We pack the family in there –five, then six, then seven – by the time my youngest brother squeaks to life, eight of us roll in a black Plymouth Valiant station wagon. In the original old Deluxe, the rear windows don't roll down, and air is scarce in the back seat on a shimmering summer day as we roll along Montauk Highway and catch the on-ramp for the Causeway, turning straight south toward glittering Atlantic beaches.

Old Montauk Highway runs parallel to the shore of Long Island's Great South Bay, west to east, ninety miles from NYC to east-island tip. Long scenic stretches of woods and wetlands, then. Now, housing and strip-malls.

Low wooden guard-rail fences sit back ten feet from the road's edge at the Causeway on-ramp. Upon those rails sit young boys with surfboards. Elbows on bare knees, one fist supporting the chin, the other hand out with thumb toward the beach. My mother with an endearing look over at my father, and him a sidelong glance, "Where'm I gonna put 'em?"

We roll up the ramp, where we get a blast of cooler salt air even before reaching the first bridge. Looking out the rear window I can no longer see the young hitchhikers, but know someone will stop for them, I'd seen it before. They'll jump off the rail and into the car, sliding their boards through side windows or out the back of a station wagon. They'll roll off toward ocean glory, away from the eyes of their parents and the stifling confinement of a sweaty back seat. I want out of that car and onto that fence rail.

I'm twelve when I first hitchhike to the beach with friends. We have no surfboards yet, so rides are especially easy to come by. A car bounces off the roadway and onto the sandy shoulder, a passenger door flies open – "Hop aboard!" We do five-mile sorties from the on-ramp to the causeway to the Captree Bridge, then over the draw bridge, then over the final span to the barrier island and the ocean shore.

Not to say I'd encourage my own kids to hitchhike today. It is a different world we make now. Just saying, I'm grateful to have had an easy, sun-decked introduction to the open road, to have survived it and been enriched. To have found that freedom easily, getting ourselves to the blessed beach on our own, made all future adventures seem reasonable. Sitting there on that long splintery rail, right arm extended, thumb out, we see sympathetic gazes in the passing car windows. Soon, someone stops to whisk us across three bridges to the continent's edge, where sunshine, salt air, and sand dunes rule, with bikini'd girls everywhere. Nary a crazed thrill-killer do we ever encounter.

Gone to Dogs

In autumn 1972 I set out on a familiar course, hitchhiking from Oneonta, New York toward Long Island. It's a trip I'd made numerous times – southeastward on Route 28 through Delhi, on to Big Indian, past Sundown just below Woodstock, and at Kingston a turn straight south toward NYC on the New York State Thruway, across the Throgs Neck Bridge and down to the south shore of my longed-for island. It's a five-hour drive, which means 7-10 (maybe 14) if you're hitchhiking. I'd had both good and bad luck on this route as vagaries of weather, world events, local custom, traffic or lack, daylight or darkness impinged upon the wiggle and flow of the finger'd road.

It's late fall with a distinct upstate chill in the air, but I'm fine with layers on, a sweatshirt over my flannel and thermals, a red-checked CPO jacket, wool hat, canvas rucksack over my shoulder. Blue jeans and insulated work boots and the beginnings of my first winter beard.

Several short hops with farmers and a mix of other generous travelers take me over Franklin

Mountain and on past Delhi. Then one of those lonely stretches of road that, as a hitchhiker, take you out of the echo chamber of your own mind and into something wider, higher, more various — Catskill Mountains leaning on all sides, quiet highway ribbon bereft of traffic but crowded with a flow of other slow distractions. Pungent tang of crushed leaves, clatter of wind in dry branches, low burbling surge of a creek below the roadside. I walk, breathing it. You feel yourself passing along an extended moment — a non-stop full stop — beautifully vacant, deep in detail, hinged with possibility.

A whine of tires breaks the spell. A small dark car lurches off onto the shoulder, sliding to a stop on gravel just ahead of me. I jog toward it, seeing through its rear window a swarm of activity inside as I get closer. The driver — a woman in her forties I guess, a tangle of long black hair streaked with gray — is herding her three large dogs out of the front seat and into the back of her small coupe. The dogs — a German Shepherd, a black Labrador, and a huge Old English Sheepdog — are reluctantly squirming to make room for the new passenger, bumping each other and grunting as they slowly spin circles and try to re-settle. As I sit down and look back at them, I see that the Shepherd is the nervous nelly of the three. When I turn around it pushes its way back into the front seat as I angle the rucksack off and try to settle myself in. The driver – Mary Ellen – extends her right hand over to me as she shoves at the Shepherd's rump with her left, barking at him, "Back – back seat Rex – back!" But he no sooner gets his forelegs into the back than he spins back around and jumps into the space between us in the front.

Rex clearly wants to ride shotgun, and once Mary Ellen jerks the car back onto the highway, he is with us to stay. This is one large Shepherd. His ample flank shoves me against the passenger door as he squirms his way into his own comfort. I glance back to see there is no room for Rex in the back now, with the other two sprawled across the back seat end-to-end, Catskill Mountains of dog fur.

By then Mary Ellen has given up on coaxing Rex and is spinning into a soliloquy, as if talking to herself, not me. Musings of winter coming, upstate life being way better than

city life even if winter blew, the damned-
crazy neighbors with the junk cars all over the
damned lot, her evil ex-husband the jerk, her
recently dearly departed dog Stanley – "Now
there was a good dog, a companion, not like this
one" – jerking a thumb toward Rex, who by
now has one haunch on my lap, staring straight
ahead at the racing pavement, breathing heavily
and issuing soft whimpers and growls. Restless
Rex is distressed at having to share his seat, shifts
his considerable dog-mass and shoves me harder
up against the door handle.

The next hour passes thus, with lead-footed
Mary Ellen careening from topic to topic as
Rex conquers more and more of my real estate.
Dog breath fogs the windows. The temperature
inside the car rises steadily, the damp air redolent
of dander.

Darkness falls as we lean into a ferocious
approach down an entrance ramp and onto the
Thruway. As she blasts us southward, veering
from lane to lane, I have thoughts of mortality,
visions of a smoking, twisted wreck full of dog
parts and human remains.

Then dearest Rex – we're close buddies by now – begins making another sort of noise. No longer a whimper, now a rumble of intestinal agitation. In his discomfort he turns himself again, now to occupy the precise center of my lap, facing me head-on, unable to watch the on-rushing road any longer. His gags and half-heaves take on more force, with his face mere inches from mine. I crane my neck to the right to get my mouth out of the direct line of fire, and hold my breath, my own stomach churning. Waving my hand and interrupting Mary Ellen's monologue, I manage to croak, "Car sick. Rex! Car sick!"

"Nooooo – !" Mary Ellen howls, "No – Rex! Noooooo!!"

By the grace of Jesus – Allah, Krishna, Buddha, the whole lot of them – Rex spins his body one more quarter turn, away from me and toward Mary Ellen, then spews a hot quart of dog vomit onto her lap. This inspires her in that blessed moment to veer across three lanes of traffic and put our little doggie coupe into a controlled skid along the highway shoulder. Before we fully stop she's flinging her door open, and with a torrent of foul language she steps one foot out of the car and commences flinging hand-fulls of Rex's late-lost lunch into the passing traffic, screaming "You naaaasty – rotten – fucking – dog!" (Fling, fling, fling, fling.)

Passing cars veer and honk, but can't avoid the desecration of their windshields. I take the opportunity to exit the coupe, take a deep breath and bid a fond farewell to the pack. My step back onto the gravel is a transition as sudden and welcome as any escape, in this case from a cramped and lurching dog breath horror show, punctuated finally by flung dog puke splashing off hurtling cars on a dark highway.

Mary Ellen turns to me with a puzzled look.
"You're getting out here?"

Deeper in the Well

I made that same hitch – Oneonta to Long Island – on many other occasions, some in the depths of winter. The sky broad and gray as the low hills would have it; road shoulders braced up with snow-piles so you'd have to walk on the pavement, jumping onto a snow bank when traffic thickens or quickens, with a duck and turn to avoid a blast of cold wind-wake.

I walk backwards, facing oncoming traffic, my thumb out, sliding and staggering on slush. It's a clumsy chore with heavy clothing and a backpack. Winter makes a hitch more rigorous, more plain simple survival – each brief ride a few miles of warm-up, then back into the chiller. Regarding it now, from a ledge of advancing age, I can hardly reckon how I did it. Things hurt less then, I guess. Youth is a buffer against discomfort, youth is just physically tougher, if emotionally uncertain. I had no fragility at that point.

This particular February trip begins with a light fair wind blowing down the road. I catch a ride with a timber trucker over Franklin Mountain, but then when he turns off onto Route-23 I stop him and get out. Route-28 is a safer bet. It has some quiet stretches but has proven a reliable route before. 23 has long godforsaken stretches where you might die and be reborn before you get your next lift.

My hunch proves solid. I get a string of quick rides that carry me through Delhi and eastward past Big Indian. Then I find a slack in the line, enjoying a slow trudge for a mile or so, past deep green stands of pine and fir, and a striking copse of tall, straight white birch trees. Another short-haul trucker, then a cheerful station wagon family, then a young kid driving a snow plow bring me to just south of Woodstock.

And that's where I strike gold – a sight I'd pray for had I been more grandiose in my aspirations. A hippie kid rattles up in a VW Kombi microbus – red-paneled glass all around with tattered curtains. It shudders to a stop and he flings open the passenger door. Hopping in, I'm doubly-gladdened to detect the faint sweet-smoke aroma of El Supremo. I'm looking around at his well-appointed hippie van while he gets us rolling and into fourth gear. Once cruising, he cradles the flat-banked steering wheel between his knees and rolls a joint from his leather tobacco pouch, keeping his eyes on the road and doing his hippie handiwork purely by touch. We save the joint for awhile as we talk. He's soft-spoken and kind, modest yet self-assured, calm and sweet-natured. "On a mission," he says with a sly smile. He's headed to Manhattan to pick up some supplies for "the guys at the house."

The house is just up a ways from Woodstock, in West Saugerties. The guys hid out there and wrote music in 1968, recording in the basement. Now, they come and go.

The supplies in question remain unquestioned. I know not to ask, but instead hang loose with this celestial kid who is deeper in his well than I, humble and plain and loving life. We ride generous conversation all the way down to the city's northern edge, finally firing up the joint as we approach the Whitestone Bridge. Our smooth, unhurried glide across the big pink Manhattan skyline features full-blast Mahler (Symphony No. 5 in C-Sharp Minor, Adagietto, 4th Movement) from an impressive

sound system that swamps out the whine of
the wheels on the bridge decks.

It is just that ride that keeps me hitching,
looking for one more just like it.

Ever Wonder...?

But no two rides are quite the same.

Fear did not reign supreme in the late 1960s and 1970s when I was doing most of my hitchhiking. I neither witnessed nor committed a single lurid murder, nor did I ever truly fear for my life. The vast majority of my rides carried the soft melodies of simple human kindness, doing someone a favor, sharing conversation, listening to good stories from colorful well-worn people.

Which is not to claim that bad stuff can't happen. A longtime friend related a version of this story from back in the summer of 1969. Fitz is a student at NYU, living the Greenwich Village post-beatnik life. Lower Manhattan is grimy, sullen and spooky, a somewhat unsettling place. But the Village is full of passers-through, not looking to settle but to make the scene and absorb the renegade flow of life on the low. It is a carnival.

Fitz meets a stunning girl in a Village bar one Friday night and falls for her face-first. Tall and willowy, bright and sweet-voiced, Inge from Sweden carries a lilting accent that freezes him in his tracks and blows him away like a hat in a windstorm. She's just arrived in the U.S., is staying in New York just this one night then she'll travel by bus to Yankton, South Dakota, where a job awaits her. In less than ten hours she'll be rolling. She and Fitz are shy and careful sweethearts for the next few hours, gently flirting over drinks, then walking slowly back to her YWCA dormitory, their prospects together doomed by circumstance. They kiss goodbye at the door – no males allowed inside – and he is moonstruck, just totally weightless in love. His feet float above the shabby streets the whole dark radiant walk home.

He awakes next morning with a new mission. Sitting at the edge of his bed he understands what he must do – go find her, join her there, live there somehow, see her every day and every night. He'll find work, or go hungry, what the hell. The love-hunger reaches all the way down him, and all the way back up, and around both sides. It rings in his ears and makes his skin tingle. A sweet sweet kiss, wet with promise.

With seventeen dollars in his pocket, he marches over to the restaurant kitchen where he works and tells them he'll be gone a week or so, hopes he'll have his job when he gets back but if not, oh well, I'm going anyway. I'm gone! There'll be money in South Dakota, he thinks, walking out the door – some way somehow. He just has to get there.

He's hitched a lot locally on Long Island. Actually walks a lot, but he'll stick out his thumb if he's going more than a few miles. He's taken rides and declined rides and knows how to make fast friends along the way. He's been in a few situations that trended weird and always used his gift of gab first, but can quickly fight if he has to, no fear of that. He makes his way as a gifted talker, a brash NYC college radical with hair to his shoulders and some strong opinions.

He packs a small shoulder bag with his toothbrush, a pair of clean underwear, and a pair of clean socks. He grabs his favored book of the moment and with the clothes on his back he heads out. He walks down Greenwich Street to Spring, and over to the West Street entrance to the Holland Tunnel, a tangle of lanes all arrowing into an arched subterranean pathway under the Hudson River.

His first ride is a business guy who jerks to a stop and honks – Fitz jumps in quickly and they zoom off toward Jersey City. The soot-tiled tunnel is a quick grimy ride leading to a drop-off at William Dickerson High School, where the businessman is heading north and Fitz wants to get onto the westward interstate. His rough reckoning of a map in a gas station has him heading west toward Scranton, and further along Interstate 70 west to Indianapolis, then a cut north toward Chicago, then west across Iowa to Sioux City, then across the Missouri River and on to Yankton, just across the Nebraska line in far-south South Dakota.

But often it's the last hundred miles that gets you, because you get that close and you want to push on to finally make it. You're energized by proximity even though that last stretch may be through the most desolate leg of the trip. For Fitz it is at Elk Point, Nebraska where he can smell her breath, sense her nearness after fifteen hundred miles of anticipation. Caution, in those circumstances, is tossed to the wind.

A beat-up panel truck pulls over and a guy in cowboy boots jumps out the passenger side door, motioning Fitz to sit between him and the driver. Without any hesitation he clambers in and steps on something on the floor, which he sees is a long-barreled handgun. The driver grunts and grins. Fitz turns to see two more guys in the back seat, and behind them a gun rack holding two rifles. Behind all that, a grimy curtain screening off the back of the truck. The two guys are half slumped over, just staring back at him, no friendly greetings of any kind, a grimace on one face and a scowl on the other, both cowboy hats pulled low.

They set off in silence, just the whirl of wheels in their ears. Wedged between the two up front and unsettled by the hard silence, everyone just looking straight ahead and not talking, Fitz thinks he'll just close his eyes and get some sleep. But then he feels something in his hair, behind his ear, and then feels it harder – a tug. One of the backseat cowboys is twirling his bony index finger through Fitz's hippie curls. Startled, he leans forward, thinks about swatting the jerk's hand, and hears the cowboys snorting laughter behind him.

After more silence, the driver finally says to him, "You from where?"

After a pause Fitz says, "New York City."

More silence, the driver staring straight ahead. Minutes are just miles, Fitz is thinking, just get me there. He hears snoring from the back seat and breathes a quiet sigh of relief, relaxing his shoulders, settling deeper into the seat and into his fatigue. Rides aren't always fun, but they get you there, you hope.

With eyelids drooping he steals another glance at the driver, who senses his attention and looks over. Their eyes meet for the first time, and Fitz begins to say, "If you're tired and want me to do some driving..."

The driver rolls his window down and spits out into the darkness, then rolls it back up and says, "Nahh, I'm doin' the drivin'."

More silence. And then, as Fitz begins to doze again, the driver says, "So, New York City – what's it like there?"

Fitz sits up. "Oh," he says, "it's pretty grimy and trashy. Lots of interesting people. Fair amount of street crime."

The driver says, "What's that? They steal the streets?"

Fitz stifles a laugh. "No, it's like some guy with a knife wanting your money, on the street."

"A knife? Not a gun?"

"Guns are pretty illegal in New York City. Lot of trouble if you get caught with one," says Fitz.

"But people do have 'em?"

"Yeah," Fitz says, "some do."

The driver rolls down the window and spits again. Then he looks over and says, "You ever wonder how it feels like to get shot?"

Fitz feels a bottle rocket of fear go off inside his chest and light up his fingertips. He's surrounded, no room to fight – feels suddenly trapped in a bad situation. The cowboy beside him is awake again and he can feel the eyes of the other two behind him.

"You ever wonder?" The driver repeats, looking at him now. "Ever wonder, New York City?"

Then he snorts a laugh and crooks his arm up to point backwards with his thumb, saying "Cuz if you have been wonderin' you can just ask them how it feels."

Ready to fight them all, Fitz whirls his head around to look back, where one of the slumping cowboys is pulling the curtain aside with a gapped smile. Behind the curtain and gun rack hang five freshly-shot wild turkeys.

With that, the driver bursts out laughing, and the two in back guffaw along with him, and the cowboy beside him nudges Fitz softly in the ribs with his elbow. The tension evaporates, everyone laughing together now, Fitz not the least.

Roads never end but sometimes stories do, slowly and sadly. After parting best wishes from his turkey-hunting jokers and more short hops, Fitz finally reaches Yankton. He spends the next two days looking for Inge everywhere, asking around town, visiting every shop and restaurant multiple times with little money to spend. She's just nowhere to be found. And on the third day he realizes the game is lost. The hitch home is a sorry slog, but he gets there.

The Composer

A focus on threats and violence misses the whole point of hitchhiking: you are banking on trust and the generosity of strangers. You are traveling for free and for freedom, paying only with your own generous good nature and trustworthiness (which you communicate from a distance, gesturally). You are offering to keep company with a driver who wants conversation, to share stories, a joke, talk politics, engage in speculation about the meaning of life or listen sympathetically to tales of hard times, loss, heartbreak. Usually you are joining company with someone who wants nothing more than to pass the miles not alone. The conversation may be articulate or inchoate, even incoherent; thoughts enlightening or half-formed; periods of silence easy, full and comfortable, or oppressive. Seated beside someone for a length of time and distance in chatter or in quietude, you will learn something about them and also about yourself. The more serene you are in your own skin, the more easily you can set another soul free, if only for a short while.

We were grateful for the time and the progress no matter who was driving. On one occasion, I team up with a buddy to hitchhike to Bar Harbor, Maine from lower Manhattan. In 1971, downtown New York is a decrepit warren of litter-strewn streets lined with deserted and part-empty commercial buildings. It's not yet safe or popularly hip to live down there, so these angular cast-iron and block buildings are sparsely populated with dying businesses, squatters, and authentic artists colonizing these huge empty spaces as cheap (or free) working studios where they can live and do their work. You have to venture far to find basic human services – a food market, somewhere to buy toilet paper. So the downtown pioneers improvise, live close to the bone, and fit out their studios with junk treasure found on the street. They haul supplies tens of blocks from the civilized neighborhoods of Midtown or Greenwich Village to the sooty vacancy of what will someday become known as SoHo and TriBeCa.

My friend Lee Krugman has a place on Hudson Street on the Lower West Side, having abandoned one in the East Village when it became just too full of scary people to tolerate any longer. He'd eventually move back to the East Village, to a tenement on Rivington Street just blocks from the Hell's Angels NYC headquarters. This is long before any of these spots are colonized by yuppies. The streets are deserted at night but for wandering junkies and lost muggers. In each of these places, Lee Krugman sets up a small working studio where he can live inexpensively, edit his 8mm films, and engage with other independent filmmakers gathering at places like the Anthology Film Archives and represented in *Film Culture* magazine – the stars including Jonas Mekas, Stan Brakhage, Peter Kubelka, Ken Kelman, and others. Lee is a young acolyte, an aspiring artist in celluloid. He makes his little films with his hands, one of which he mangled in a snow blower in his youth.

Lower Manhattan – and NYC generally – is hot, smelly, rank, and angry in the summertime. The atmosphere is both pissed off and redolent of piss. It's hard to evoke that place and time without engaging all of the senses – I do remember this clearly: emerging squeaky clean and revitalized from a cold shower after a sweaty night, getting dressed and walking off down the street, and by the second block feeling dirty again. Your sweat forms a sort of thin mud on your skin, bearing a distinct post-industrial tang. All the girls, and presumably the guys, smelled and tasted like that.

So for us, with no car and little cash, summertime NYC is all about planning an escape and making a break for it. Our chance comes on a hot Sunday in early August, when we feel we might just auto-combust if we don't get out. The cool summer air of southern Maine seems like a worthy goal. Hitching is our only option, so we pack rucksacks with bare essentials, take the A train all the way up to Inwood, and walk past Isham Hill Park and across the Broadway Bridge, then catch a ride further up Broadway to Van Cortlandt Park and onto the Henry Hudson Parkway. Now on unfamiliar ground, we dead-reckon our way east and catch several short hops that take us over toward the Connecticut border. With rising elation we find our way out of the tangle of New York's northern suburbs and highways – Connecticut is New England, right? Almost Maine?

Once in Connecticut, we make our way onto an entrance ramp for I-95 North and sit there awhile, thumbs out, before catching another series of short hops – in the back of a pickup truck, in the cab of a dump truck, and in a van with a hippie family. With every mile we put between ourselves and lower Manhattan our spirits lighten – never mind that the south shore of Connecticut can also be hot as blazes in the summertime. But the escape and forward progress are renewing us, mile by mile. The smile on Lee's face is one I'd not seen in many a day.

Somewhere near Stamford, the afternoon heat is just beginning to yield to an on-shore breeze from the Long Island Sound. We stand side by side at this highway spot, near a gas station, for quite some time. The long day is beginning to weigh on us, and we face a classic hitchhiker's dilemma: our spot is good, with an easy place for cars to pull over, yet it's yielding nothing but wary glances and an occasional middle finger from passing drivers. Do we pull up stakes and hike up ahead? Will we find a better spot? Will we wind up at a terrible spot, with no easy place to stop, but someone will stop anyway? We mull the decision to stay or go. I imagine early pioneers, exhausted from rougher travel, facing similar decisions: drop camp here, or keep going?

Will we find something better? Or will we find hungry bears? Here or somewhere else, what will come? It's a moment to test mental toughness, to trust instinct, trust your gut. In these situations, you block out doubt and listen hard for that little voice that offers a workable answer.

We decide to move. No matter how good this spot is, it just isn't working. Our luck feels like it's hardening like food left on a plate. We hike on ahead, trudging along disconsolate, walking with our backs to the traffic, our left thumbs out – not usually a winning tactic. But after about a mile, lo and behold, a sedan heaves over onto the shoulder and an arm emerges from the driver's window, waving us in.

We don't jog to the car, we sprint. Approaching it, Lee reaches to open the front passenger side door but the driver, an older gent, waves us both into the back seat. At a glance, we see he has something big and boxy beside him on the front seat, and thus no room for us there. We happily open the rear doors and jump in, no hesitation. With two of us and one old man, we have little concern. The big back seat has plenty of room for us and our packs. We sigh in deep relief.

Lee is first to speak. "How far are you going, sir?"

He gets no immediate answer. The old man doesn't seem to hear him, is gazing at us intently in the rear-view mirror as he drives. Now he speaks up. "Where you boys tryin' to get to?"

"Boston," I say. "Or further north – Bar Harbor."

"Ay?" he says. "Boston? Well you boys are in luck. I'm headin' all the way up to Maine!" He's pleased and proud to deliver this good news, and Lee and I look at each other slack-jawed. Moving from that damned perfect spot delivered us into the arms of salvation. We can hardly contain our joy.

"Ay?" the old man says again. "That good enough?"

"It's better than good enough, sir," I say, and we take turns thanking him profusely, but his squint in the rear-view tells us he's still having trouble hearing us. On closer inspection we can see that he was quite old indeed, with deep neck wrinkles, flaky dried skin on his ears, and sparse gray hair that bears the uneven texture of bad haircuts. He wears rimless glasses with frames that wrap around both ears, making them stick out.

"Ay?" he says again, although we'd said nothing. So we lean forward in our seats and put our arms up against the back of his, the better to converse.

"You boys have jobs?" he asks, and I respond first, speaking almost in a shout. "Yessir, I drive a delivery truck, and I also have a part-time factory job." He nods, showing he heard me this time.

"And how about you?" he aims his reflected gaze at Lee, who clears his throat and takes a deep breath to add volume. "I work in film," Lee says.

"You what?"

"I'm... I work in film production. I do camera work and I make my own films."

"Where you do that?" the old man asks, skeptical.

"New York," Lee says, shifting a bit. "I work in lower Manhattan."

"Not Hollywood?" the old guy asks, his incredulity rising with the squinches in his nose. "Don't they make the movies in Hollywood?"

Lee squirms some more. "I don't make those kinds of movies. I make small movies, in Super-8 millimeter, sometimes 16."

The driver shakes his head and frowns, not quite buying it, but then his face brightens. "If you need a musical soundtrack, you just let me know. I'm a composer!"

That brings us both up short. It's not what we're expecting to hear from this odd old bird. Lee has just given me an album by Philip Glass, whom he'd heard perform in the East Village. Called *Music in Similar Motion,* I'd found it at first frustrating then fascinating. Glass was making his mark in Manhattan and elsewhere performing and recording hypnotic, repetitive, minimalist compositions. He and his quartet progressed from subway busking and performances at downtown lofts to galleries and museums, where the strange repetitions with minor variations could be more accessible, or at least palatable, to free-range audiences over those trapped in seats.

We're at a creative intersection here, it seems. "What sort of music do you compose?" Lee asks him.

"Want to hear some?" the Composer says, reaching over to the box beside him. It's then we see he has a large reel-to-reel tape deck on the seat beside him, large even by standards of the day. Surely vacuum tube driven, it seems to be jerry-rigged along with a large speaker on the floor to the car's electrical system, with a cable snaking up under the dashboard.

When he hits the PLAY button we experience one of those musical moments that instantly freeze your brain, a function of both an unsafe volume and the unexpected nature of the music itself. It's what might be described as very loud Roller-rink Music. The melodies are simple, repetitive, evoking flocks of circling swans on roller skates or ice skates, with overtones of cotton candy, circus sideshow, and adolescent sexual frisson under layers of wool clothing.

Dumbstruck, we listen as our driver hums along, drumming bent fingers on the steering wheel. We avoid each others' eyes as the Composer steals satisfied glances at us in the rear-view, his eyebrows hopping with how-about-that pride. We spend the next several hours in happy but very loud harmony, choking down laughter and, when we can't choke any more, we laugh and clap. This gleefully torturous soundtrack gets us where we're bound to go, all the way to Maine, and once we're out of the car we torture ourselves further with writhing laughter, our heads ringing.

It's pure deliverance – what you get to get where you get to. The Maine air makes it all the more wondrous, like cotton candy you can breathe. And sweet silence.

The Fates

I did most of my hitchhiking in the 1960s and 1970s, when it was still a common practice and I was still a teenager, and knew myself to be indestructible.

But that bulletproof sense was tested on a short local hitch – a ride to the beach in 1968 – with three friends, Artie, Murray, and Cunaz. All three were talented musicians riding the 1960s wave of rock & roll garage bands as well as school band and orchestra. Artie was repeatedly castigated for smoking cigars during orchestra practice, but usually given a pass by virtue of his sheer talent – he could pick up any instrument and just play it. Their rock band gigged in a dark little bar that featured a hijacked piano with the words PROPERTY OF WEST ISLIP PUBLIC SCHOOLS stenciled across its backboard. It had been rolled to the bar on its hard little wheels after a break-in at a nearby elementary school.

The bar has a tiny coat-check room beside the front entrance. If Dennis is working the coat check and you leave a ten dollar bill in your coat pocket, you'll find a lid of grass (an unweighed ounce) when you get your coat.

On this sunshiny day I'm off to body-surf waves and gaze at bikinis, not due at work until that evening. I no sooner stick out my thumb than along come Artie, Murray, and Cunaz in Artie's mom's station wagon. I hop in back with Cunaz and immediately detect the sweet scent of El Supremo, the boys having fired up a fat joint moments earlier. I'm still novice to that trade, but then, we all are. We're in high school, as they call it, and just learning to fly. I gladly accept the joint when it's passed and take a hit as the other three giggle and carry on, jabbering like drunk monkeys.

I settle in for the ride, enjoying the lift-off, chit-chatting with Cunaz about a girl we both know and hope to see at the beach in her skinny bikini. Artie steers us onto the bay bridge while he and Murray mock-argue over who is the better driver. Murray maintains that since he's been stealing cars since he was twelve – an older cousin having taught him how to hot-wire at a tender age – he can credibly claim the title of Best Driver In This Car.

Artie shakes his head from side to side as he rolls us toward the bridge's arch at ever-increasing speed. "Fool!" Murray screeches, "Pull this piece of crap over and I'll show you some driving!" With nowhere to pull over on the narrow two-lane bridge suspended eighty feet over the Great South Bay, Artie does the next best thing: he lets go of the steering wheel and jumps into the back seat, landing head-first between Cunaz and me, stomping the car roof with both feet as he slumps there upside-down, shouting "Go ahead and drive, then!"

Time slows at such moments, even at 80MPH. Murray casually reaches over and grabs the wheel just as we're beginning to veer, then slides over, turns completely around to give us his best Alfred E. Newman smile, then whips his head back and punches the car up toward 100MPH on the downhill side of the bridge. Despite our weed buzz, or maybe because of it, Cunaz and I remain remarkably calm through all this, grinning like sphinxes with Artie squirming between us. My heart races later, lying on the sand, looking up and thinking back. We are not indestructible, but with luck we survive young efforts to send our parents into life-long grief.

As things turn out, we back-seat passengers fare better in the long run. I'm sitting here in a shady street-side Barcelona cafè, near fifty years later, writing this. Still restless, still traveling, but not usually hitchhiking near or far, now. It's nice to kick back now and reflect on the easy freedom and exhiliaration of those younger times, all the risk and reward balancing good/bad luck with good/bad decision.

Way back then, Cunaz had the great good fortune to be immortalized in a moment of luck and wonder, his face appearing on the original Woodstock album cover, the back side, crowd shot, smack-dab in the middle, looking up with his high-beam smile. You can't miss him.

The other two met harsher fates. Murray was convicted of arson-for-hire (his side-gig) after being captured fleeing the scene of a burning restaurant in a full-leg cast resulting from his crash of a stolen motorcycle a week earlier. Murray rose to the position of musical director of the Attica State Prison band a few years after the uprising.

Meanwhile Artie, the true musical genius of the bunch, spiraled upwards and then quickly down. At 19, he'd been playing guitar in a club in Manhattan, sitting in with pros on a regular basis. One night he was offered airfare and travel cash to fly to Oakland and audition for Tower of Power. While Artie's there, someone doses him with too much LSD, a bender from which he never fully returns. His parents fly out to Oakland and bring him back to New York to a state hospital, this bright young musical buddha gone to ashes.

It's rare for a hitch to have that kind of coda, but there it is. It all might have ended differently for each of us but for the graces of fate, which can drift across lanes of good and bad fortune like a runaway car sometimes.

The Flying Car

The most authentic danger in hitchhiking may not be what we'd expect – the serial killer, cruising predator, or chain-saw kidnapper. I've turned down rides most often when a driver seemed drunk, hopelessly high, vague when asked where they were going, or otherwise incapable of simply driving the vehicle safely. The clearest and most present danger in hitching is the same one we all face whenever we get into a car: driving accidents in the U.S. claim almost 100 lives every day, with tens of thousands of souls lost to traffic accidents every year. Those numbers dwarf things we tend to fear more: double the number of murders, and 1,200 times the annual average number of U.S. terrorism victims. The most serious threat to any hitchhiker is the simple fact that they are climbing into a car driven by another human being.

When a young driver doing 80MPH over a two-land bridge jumps into the back seat – well, we were very fortunate to survive those antics. That same bridge is part of a string of three bridges that carry people in cars from

Long Island's south shore across the Great South
Bay, then the State Channel that cuts below
Captree Island, then the Fire Island Inlet. Not
long after my lucky ride with Artie, Murray and
Cunaz, another group of kids is cruising at high
speed along that same route. It's after midnight,
and unknown to them, another group of kids
has managed to break into the control tower
of the bascule drawbridge spanning the State
Channel, and raise the bridge decks to a near-
twenty-degree tilt. Whether the car's occupants
even notice the raised bridge deck before they
hit it is not known – the driver didn't brake or
skid. The car is launched across the span, with
the sole survivor ejected as it flies. She lands
on the leading edge of the opposite deck and
manages to cling to the steel frame, sixty feet
above the roiling water of the channel, until
help finally arrives. She hangs on for dear life
despite a broken arm, ribs, and leg. And she later
remembers nothing of the launch or impact
– only the minute-by-minute desperation of
cold hard steel, salt air, stabbing pain with each
breath, and what she can only know as a cruel
and unreasonable end to her short, sweet life.
She does survive, but as the only survivor she is
ever-after haunted by the guilt, regret, and the

understanding that bad things happen fast. You never see them coming.

So often, we fear the wrong things. Hitchhiking is unsafe for all sorts of reasons, but you can be prepared to ward off some of those; the greater dangers, like car wrecks, are more mundane. We're best at tuning those ones out.

So how do we keep ourselves safe? Unless we're truly desperate, we check out the driver and car before getting in, and we learn to do this efficiently and fearlessly. If there's going to be trouble, let it happen there on the roadside rather than inside a speeding car or in some remote place. We try not to be outnumbered. We avoid sitting between the driver and another passenger, avoid being surrounded. We keep our pack near at hand – usually on our lap – to both protect it and have it handy as a shield or weapon. Whenever possible, we sit by a door we can open. Most importantly, we keep up the banter and make ourselves fully human to the driver, and show real interest in their humanity and their story. We're always ready to act, to answer any aggression with a fast and furious escalation of aggression, verbal and physical –

the mindset being, if there is going to be a fight, let's fight right now. Aggressors will often back down if you out-aggress and out-crazy them. The basic formula for dealing with any bully is that they are acting that way out of weakness, not strength, so if you must respond to bullying, go hard, right at that weakness. There are no guarantees of safety in anything you do, but fast courage can work, and is one option when uncertainty trends towards threat.

Happily, I had no physical altercation on any hitch. A few times I have to talk hard and tough, and be ready to fight, but never have to throw a punch. Most often things settle easily into basic chit-chat, with curiosity and kindness. As long as boundaries are respected, I'm fine. I'm a good listener. And a sympathetic ear can make a better day for a bored traveler.

Fuzzy's Index Finger

Union Boulevard runs east-west, parallel to the Long Island Railroad tracks. It used to be my father's favorite route anywhere. If you couldn't get there via Union Street, it wasn't worth going.

Back when our neighbor Walter (we called him Fuzzy) moved his young family out to the wilds of suburban Long Island, circa 1955, they were city folk from the Bronx, he a Polish Catholic, his wife Florence, Jewish and given to fits of what they used to call hysteria. They had a young son, and then a daughter two years later. As city people, they did not own a car; they'd always had public transit within easy reach. But in the wilds of newly-suburbanizing Long Island, the only public transit of the time were the Bay Shore railroad station (4 miles to the east) to the Babylon railroad station (4 miles west), and from there into Brooklyn and Manhattan. Both of these train stations were entry points for hundreds, then thousands, then tens of thousands of workday commuters to and from New York City, mornings and evenings.

Fuzzy faced a dilemma, having no car but needing to get to Babylon railroad station every morning for the train commute to his job in the city. His normal method for making that trip was to stand on the shoulder of Union Street, twenty feet from the railroad tracks, in his suit and tie and fedora with his briefcase, and hitchhike. Being a unique sort of fellow, Fuzzy eschewed the customary hitchhiking gesture of arm down and thumb out, instead crooking his arm up with his hand beside his face, index finger pointing in the direction he was headed, lit by a smile.

Day by day, it works. Commuters stop and pick him up, spirit him away to Babylon station. Fuzzy holds a convincing pose as a businessman, well-dressed and put together. But in conversation he prefers to discuss his theories as a self-styled UFO expert (he pronounces it "oo-foes") and take small talk in that direction. He claims to have seen little green men with glassware on their heads in his backyard, which borders ours.

Fuzzy devises other strategies for overcoming his lack of wheels. When running errands on the weekends he'll hitchhike to Babylon village, go to the A&P supermarket and load up on groceries. Then he leaves his grocery bags up front by the manager's office and marches down the block to one of several car dealerships in the area. He spends a minute perusing a shiny new model in the parking lot, peering in the windows, until a salesman hustles out to greet him, at which point Fuzzy announces that he intends to buy this car and requests a test drive. The salesman hustles back inside to get the keys, sensing a quick hook. When he returns, Fuzzy asks the salesman to drive, which is a bit unusual but not unheard-of; the salesman gets behind the wheel, Fuzzy takes the passenger seat and directs the salesman to the A&P store, where he asks the salesman to pull over and "wait here for a moment." He fetches his grocery bags, loads them into the back seat, and directs the salesman towards his home. Upon arrival there, he again asks the salesman to "wait here for a moment" while he carries the grocery bags into the house. Then he returns to tell the salesman that he will not, in fact, be buying this car today – the ride is not smooth enough. The salesman by now knows he's been taken for a ride.

Fuzzy repeats this routine numerous times. When he's worn out his welcome at one car dealership he moves on to the next. In time, of course, everyone at all of the dealerships knows who he is and what he's up to, and they demur when he asks for a test drive. And so Fuzzy then has to resort to hitchhiking to the A&P and hitchhiking back home with his grocery bags, which is cumbersome at best, and most difficult in poor weather – brown paper grocery bags tend to tear easily when wet.

Comes the day that Fuzzy takes a taxi to the Ford dealership in Babylon. The salesmen see him and roll their eyes. He strides across the sales floor where he is informed "no free rides today, pal" to which he replies, "Today, I will buy a car" and he pulls an envelope stuffed with cash from his jacket. He signs the necessary paperwork and asks to take a test drive, but this time he will be driving. Given the stack of cash on the barrelhead, they put Fuzzy behind the wheel of a brand new white Mercury station wagon with faux wood paneling and a bright red interior – steering wheel, dashboard, seats, carpet, clock, everything in dressed in bright red leather. It soon becomes apparent that Fuzzy's driving skills are rudimentary – the salesman takes him on a brief but exciting test drive out one side of the parking lot and back in the other side, perhaps 1/16th of a mile in total. There are several near-misses along the way but they manage to get the car back intact and hand him the keys. Fuzzy lurches off homeward in his spanking-new white Mercury wagon.

The lack of driving experience soon leads to problems. Fuzzy has a particularly hard time backing the car out of the driveway. On his first attempt, heading off to Babylon station the next Monday morning, he fails to notice a large garbage truck parked at the end of the driveway, picking up his trash. He puts his briefcase into the car, gets in, starts it up, and throws it into reverse. Two garbagemen dive out of his way as he cracks into the side of their truck. The station wagon, being a stout steel vehicle of the time, suffers only cosmetic damage.

But soon, there is a similar accident – this time, Fuzzy backs out into traffic without looking and the Mercury is hit on its rear quarter-panel by a passing car. Again, little significant damage, but this time police are called to the scene. They note that this odd fellow seems to have little awareness of the rules of the road.

The final straw is drawn on a fine workday morning when Fuzzy backs into a school bus waiting at the end of his driveway, picking up his neighbors' children and his own. The authorities takes this incident more seriously and he is relieved of his driver's license.

So in that very short span of time, with the Mercury's odometer not yet turning 200 miles, and with various dings and dents, the car is parked in the driveway and Fuzzy resumes his normal hitchhiking and taxi-taking. The family begins using the Mercury as a sort of clubhouse and Sunday morning lounge – they come out of the house in their pajamas, loaded down with the Sunday newspapers, and sit in the car to read the funnies to each other, shrieking and howling. When they're done they sling the papers onto the rear deck of the station wagon. This is a weekly routine for an extended period of time, until the back of the car fills up with newspapers, then fills up beyond full, and the rear end of the Mercury begins to sag noticeably. In time the rear end of the car gives out under the weight of so much paper, and one day a tow truck appears, drags the car backwards down the length of the driveway, then forward to its final resting place.

Fuzzy never owns another automobile, but years later his son does. Kevin buys a used car of a model typically used as police cars and turns it into a faux police cruiser, complete with radio antennas and a revolving light. He does not have an actual siren but makes siren noises by sticking his head out the window and wailing. Kevin is detained by police after pulling several drivers over and writing them faux tickets from a little note pad he carries. Eventually that car is also rendered legally unusable, and sits in the driveway for some years.

There should be a bronze statue beside the railroad tracks of Fuzzy hitchhiking with his index finger, smiling toward Babylon.

Young Kyle

My friend Kyle began his hitchhiking career when he was young, catching local rides in his mid-teens then longer ones a few years later, often solo, sometimes with a buddy. We sat one night and he related a few of his stories, as he tells them below.

I did a bunch of hitchhiking between 1974 and 1979. At the beginning of this period I was about fifteen years old, then nineteen or twenty at the end.

Those years were lively ones in the United States. I grew up reading *On the Road,* I think a friend of mine told me about it in seventh grade, when I was twelve. He said, you gotta read this book, and handed it to me in homeroom. I fell into it, and kept falling for several days. It blew me away completely.

As a junior high school kid in a New Jersey suburb, reading *On the Road* at that point was a revelation. I had a turbulent childhood, my parents were divorced – not a terrible situation by some standards, but a bit mixed up, confusing. *On the Road* got through to me in a certain way during that time. By 1970 the sixties had happened, and we were at the end of the start of the hippie era, the first hippie era. Counterculture had grown quickly but was beginning to devolve and decay, while also settling into the margins of the mainstream. The big anti-war Moratorium and the Kent State killings happened right around that time. I recall feeling distant from the news I was watching on television – somehow apart from it. I was too young to fully participate, but more and more began wanting to. A few years earlier Martin Luther King had been killed, then Bobby Kennedy. Distant from me on a TV screen, and hard to believe. The 1968 election campaigns, Chicago, the Vietnam war at its height – all of these big events seemed to be turning on their own energy, but not mine.

Somehow reading *On the Road* around that time, it struck me – wow, this is saying something exciting, in a way that makes it participatory for me, and not just spectator sport. This is the idea of counterculture, and maybe that is a better way to go – rather than following the people saying, "My country, right or wrong – my country, love it or leave it," what Nixon liked to call "the great Silent Majority." No, I thought now, it's not your way or the highway – it's a new way down the highway! My country, love it and go find it.

There was powerful sense of romance in that book that caught me right away. Maybe one reason – my Dad had taken me on a short hitch-hike, near where we were on a short vacation in Florida, when I was six years old. It remained then, and remains now, a vivid memory that Kerouac brought back to me.

I was little, but recall it clearly. We were staying on a boat belonging a friend of my Dad's down in Fort Lauderdale. That, of course, was a great kick in itself. And one day my Dad wants to go to see a new James Bond movie playing in town, but we don't have a car. So he says, "We'll just hitchhike there!" He says, "We won't have any trouble getting a ride, cause you're six. And when people see you out there, they'll pick us up." And he was right! So we hitchhiked to and from that movie, and from then on I never had any negative association with hitchhiking – it was a benign experience, and kind of wondrous to me. So combine that with, later, being bewitched by *On the Road,* and I was never afraid to go do it.

Aside from local hitches, the first big solo hitchhiking journey I remember was in 1974. I came out from New Jersey to Kenyon College in central Ohio as a prospective student. I didn't have enough money to fly both ways – this was in the days before airline deregulation and fares were higher. I had enough money to fly from Newark to Columbus, but not enough to fly home. I think the plan was that I would take a bus home, which back then was much cheaper than flying. I was fifteen at the time, and it was November.

On the bus from the Columbus airport to a drugstore in Mount Vernon, near Kenyon, my luggage vanished. So there I was without my suitcase, courtesy of Greyhound.

So absent my luggage I come up to Kenyon, to meet my host students. I go to my interview the next day wearing a flannel shirt and bluejeans, apologizing that I don't have better clothing on. The Dean of Admissions doesn't seem to care.

When it was time to leave the next day, somehow Greyhound found the suitcase I got it back.

So when I was preparing to leave Kenyon on Sunday I went for a dining hall brunch and sat with a crew of freshmen, all very impressed with themselves in their worldliness, given I was a few years younger than the typical prospective student. They were asking how I was going to return home to New Jersey.

So I said, "I'm going take a bus home from Mount Vernon if I can just get there." I would later learn that a few years back it was easy to get back and forth between Kenyon College and nearby Mount Vernon, because there was a ride bench you could go to, a politely structured form of hitchhiking. You'd go sit on the ride bench – there was one on campus and another in Mount Vernon – and people stopped and picked you up, took you back or forth.

But one of my young advisors, this rich kid from Long Island, says "Oh, don't take the bus. Why don't you just hitchhike home?"

I don't know if he was serious or just just being an asshole, or if he was daring me, or baiting me, or what it was. But for some reason, in my fifteen-year-old brain, lit by Jack Kerouac and memories of my father, it seemed like a good idea. I'd hitchhike home with my little brown American Tourister suitcase.

I stood down at the base of the hill that leads up to Kenyon and stuck my thumb out. I don't recall details of the rides for the first couple of hours because I'm not sure how well I knew how to get back to New Jersey – and I was somewhat preoccupied with figuring that out.

Later I became very familiar with those routes because I traveled them back and forth with other students many times, but at that time I was too young to drive and I'd never made the trip before as a passenger. I knew I had to get back to Northwest Jersey, where my Dad lived in Hackettstown just off Route 80. And I somehow got a string of rides that got me up to Route 80 on the border of Ohio and Pennsylvania, up around Youngstown.

There I was, standing roadside with my suitcase, trying to thumb a ride, and I catch a great one. I get picked up by a guy in a full-sized van, which was almost filled with cases of Coors beer he's bringing from Colorado to the east coast, which was a thing back then. It was considered highly cool in New York and Boston to have a cold Coors can in your hand. It wasn't distributed east of the Rockies, so if you wanted it, you had to go get it. Or buy some from a friend who made the trip.

So Mister Coors picks me up and takes me all the way across Pennsylvania, all day and into the night. I'm in my prime, drinking Coors with this guy who doesn't care how old I am, talking shit and laughing. I get progressively inebriated as we go, and eventually surrender my navigational duties to the pilot. Coors takes me all the way to my Dad's house and drops me off drunk, late that night – no coming in and introducing himself, he beats it out of there, the anonymous Good Samaritan. It was a fabulous ride, very enjoyable and surprising. And just one of those most-common hitchhiking situations – he was looking for company and easygoing chatter, I was looking to get home.

It worked out great. Lots of times I'd get rides from guys who were going a distance and just wanted someone to talk to. Some of those guys were great talkers. You'd get them rolling and they'd talk the whole time. Kerouac writes about that a bit, that sense of needing to stay awake, to do your part as conversation partner for those truck drivers.

When I think about these trips now, I recall the role of altered states of consciousness and hitchhiking. I think it has a special place there, because when you're hitchhiking, even then you're doing something that's not strictly legal. You've crossed a line and you're doing something that most people don't do.

People talk about how alcohol is liquid courage, the way they gave rum to the sailors and soldiers going into battle. For our little hitchhiking army in the late 70s, marijuana was our rum. There's something about these adventures – my life back then was involved on and off with smoking marijuana for the change of consciousness it created, the shift that made life more interesting, and ever-so-much-more-so.

Somehow getting into these hitchhiking situations – although they put you into this alternate reality where I wouldn't say that everything was always good – sometimes it could make you nervous – it could make you worry more about situations, but also make them seem weirder, and somehow also made them seem cooler. This is a real adventure! I'm doing this thing! I'm actually sitting here in the cab of a truck with somebody I don't know, driving across Indiana. Like Kerouac! And I'm stoned! Wow!! Look how cool the road looks and the rest areas and the sun glinting off the windshield and how dirty the windshield is and how this guy just bounces up and down every time we hit a bump – comical! It was very seductive, an engaging state of mind. I was pleasantly cut loose much of the traveling time.

I think there is a pretty close correlation there between the road and getting high. It takes you down different avenues regarding human consciousness and our ability to deal with each other. And how we people relate to each other when we're in altered states as opposed to being straight. I think one of the problems is that the altered states, even today, have this kind of taboo feeling to them, that people are a little ashamed to talk about, or reluctant, even though it's so common today. People are still guarded, even though clearly things have changed in terms of the legal penalties for small amounts of pot. One of the interesting things about it is that you have these experiences that seem very profound at the time. And then once you're straight, you think, that wasn't very profound. Or, you have these great ideas that completely dissipate in the light of day. But I have to say – I still don't know which was the truth. Because maybe I did have great insights and just couldn't hold onto them – as if, once you remove the stoned state, there is a realm that's now out of reach.

In the summer of 1976 I was working various jobs back in New Jersey, and I talked to a friend of mine from high school about hitchhiking to California. We decided then and there, we were going. I don't know why he was willing to do it, but he was.

Barry was two years older than me and had graduated high school in 1974. So he was over eighteen at the time, and I was seventeen. We'd done some local traveling with dreams of longer and wider adventure. We put together some gear over that summer – good backpacks, tents, sleeping bags. We packed along some food and water, the supplies we'd need to pitch camp on the side of a road or out there anywhere we were stranded.

Our plan was to hitchhike to California at the end of the summer when we finished our summer jobs. There and back. Over the summer we saved money for college – he was at Johns Hopkins, I was at Kenyon – and we both had some extra money, a couple hundred dollars each. That would get us round trip to the far coast and home.

We both somehow managed to get our parents to okay this, we didn't just sneak off and do it. We had some friends from high school who were living in California, which somehow helped make all this more palatable to the parents. These friends-of-the-family were up in Sonoma County in a town called Healdsburg, which back then was just a dumpy little agricultural town about 70 miles north of San Francisco. Now it's wine country.

We hit the road on the first or second week of August. Barry's parents took us into Manhattan, to the Port Authority bus terminal, where we could catch a bus out of the metro area and onto some highways. We didn't want to start hitchhiking at the Lincoln tunnel, where traffic is more complicated and rides less likely.

So we take a Greyhound to Mount Pocono, Pennsylvania. It's right on Route 80, the major east-west interstate. The bus stop is less than a mile from Route 80, which is great, but our timing is less than great. By the time we get off the bus it's 10PM, and it takes us awhile to walk from the bus station to the highway. We begin hitching there in the dark of night, in the middle of nowhere, in the Pocono Mountains, surrounded by vast wilderness. It just goes to show what a couple of young ninnies we were.

So we stand there at the Route 80 entrance ramp out of Mount Pocono and stick our thumbs out, and needless to say, the next couple of hours are long ones. This is the bad part of hitchhiking – it can have stretches of time where you hang in limbo. There are good days, when the rides come one after another, and there are times when it seems like an eternity without a ride, one you think might never end.

There are also, on the good days, a mix of good rides and bad ones.

But that night, for us, like Kerouac with his Hearthside dream of taking U.S. 6 all the way across the country in 1948, our Hearthside dream is to take Route 80 all the way to San Francisco. But it doesn't happen that night.

I remember lying in a ditch that very first night in Pennsylvania, looking at the sky and wondering what I've done while Barry takes his turn up on the road with his thumb out. In the years since, I've driven past that spot at least fifty times, each time nodding to myself for surviving that lost night while giving the place the finger.

We're just outside a big truck stop on the north side of the highway, near the westbound ramp – an easy place for someone to stop. But nobody will pick us up. We decide we'd be less threatening with just one of us hitching, with the other lying down in the ditch. We take turns. Down in the ditch you try to relax and rest, but it's not such a restful place. That goes on for awhile, taking turns, until someone finally picks us up – a short ride, but it gets us off that spot. We get another short ride, then a decent long ride from a trucker in a huge Kenworth truck. He's headed to Chicago with his load and he's a talker, happy to pick us up.

We both sit up front in the cab seats with him, plenty of room there for three of us after throwing our backpacks into his bed area behind us. We had not brought along any weed, fearing we'd get busted for hitchhiking plus a drug offense, a very bad scenario. But our Kenworth driver has some so we happily get stoned with him. It's quite thrilling to go across the Indiana toll road that high up – really exciting to be up there bouncing along, seeing everything from really high in both respects. Morning brings a nice clear August day and the trucker is really pleasant, keeps talking to us in a jovial conversational way, telling stories. It's just great.

So then we come into the Chicago area and at one point as we're cruising down the Dan Ryan on the South side of Chicago the driver gets a little agitated with traffic and says, "Here!" and he throws his Rand McNally National Road Atlas in my lap. "I gotta get off at 35th and Halstadt," he says. It's a yard area for bulk shipping containers with a bunch of truck terminals all around there, right off the highway. For some reason he wants me to navigate using this book of maps, but I'm too stoned to do it. On his weed! I try, but I can't make heads or tails out of where we are on the road. And so I finally just say, I can't do it.

He gets angry now and says to me, "What are you, a girl? You can't read a fucking map?" He is kind of fuming and I feel ashamed of myself. Thereafter I made a point of learning how to read maps and be a better navigator.

Anyway, we just keep going up the Dan Ryan and onto Eden's Expressway, and at some point he says, "Well shit, we're way past it. Way past it. I've gotta double back so I'm just gonna drop you guys off here." And he pulls the truck over at an exit to let us off.

After we jump down from the truck Barry says to me, "You know, I have a friend from camp who lives near here somewhere, in Wilmette. Let me call Josh and see if it's anywhere nearby." And so he makes the call from a payphone and Josh's mother answers and says, "Why yes, you're not far from our house. What – are you doing?" He says, "Well, we're hitchhiking across the country and we just got dropped off here." And she brightens and says, "Well, you have to come stay at our house!" So she picks us up and we stay very comfortably at their house that night.

This sort of dumb luck thing happens with surprising frequency. The milk of human kindness is a wondrous thing, and it happens when you are moving ahead, out there, and you're open to it. It does tend to happen when you have an expectation it will.

So the next day we take the train, lock up our stuff at the bus station and do some sightseeing around Chicago, then off to the Museum of Science and Industry, nerds that we were. Then faced with the same escape-from-New-York dilemma now in Chicago, where it's difficult to hitchhike out, we decide to hop a bus to

Omaha and get through that night that way, then start hitchhiking from Omaha in the morning, in daylight.

We have a pleasant ride that night – way better than lying in a ditch. We roll through some cool thunderstorms, and sit and talk a lot. That's my first long ride on a Greyhound bus across dark, flat Illinois, then Iowa, then down into Omaha. We get there about six in the morning and hoist our backpacks to set off walking from the bus station across a dismal part of Omaha. We put our thumbs out to snag a ride and this guy pulls over in a huge 1950s-era sedan, this long heavy car, an ugly brown color. The driver is also large – way overweight and bald – and we can now see his back seat is full of debris.

He says, "You guys want a ride?"

"Yeah," we say, "we do want a ride."

And he asks, "Where you going?"

I say, "We're heading north of San Francisco."
He says, "Well hell – I'm headed to Santa Rosa!"

So we're thinking, wow! Santa Rosa! That's practically our destination, and here we are only in Omaha. One long hop is a hitchhiker's dream. Usually.

So we get in and at first this is a really good ride despite the fact that this guy is acting just a little weird. The car is reasonably comfortable with room for all our stuff in the back on top of his debris. And our driver seems harmless, maybe just a bit odd. So we start across Nebraska and there's a song I remember from a band called Free Hot Lunch, something about I wish they'd build a bridge across Nebraska because it just goes on forever.

At that time there were Stuckey's restaurants about every 20 miles across the state, and so we're stuck, you're stuck, we're all stuck in Nebraska and our driver, we're now realizing, is no speed demon. In fact he was slow to start, and as the miles go on, he gets slower. And slower. He's drinking shorty beers and eating pills out of a bottle and driving slower and slower. So here we are – still moving west, but not rapidly.

And as he continues to slow, our driver starts talking, and it starts to become clear that this guy has mental problems. He's animated then silent, with bursts of nonsensical statements. I don't know exactly what is going on, but it isn't comforting. Not yet fully scary, but not reassuring either.

So we slowly make it all the way to Eastern Wyoming, where he wants to stop for the night. We roll into a ramshackle commercial campsite off the highway, check in and pitch our tents. And once we're all outside the car our driver begins to act weirder. It's hard to describe but something changed or became amplified in his mannerisms. My friend and I are darting looks at him and each other, getting a bit scared now. Neither of us know anything about pedophiles, that was not something we worried about, but we can tell this guy isn't quite right. So we sleep with our knives out in our sleeping bags just in case we need them. We really think we might. As he's going into his tent to sleep, our driver says, "I'll wake you two up when I'm ready to go in the morning." So we turn in too and through the fog of restless fears we suddenly notice – it's a beautiful night out there! Here we are, camping in the middle of Wyoming, with every star in the universe shining down upon us. We're awed by it.

We soon fall asleep but not for long. Our driver is ready to go at four in the morning and wakes us. We rise to the realization that we have no desire to get up at four in the morning, and more so, no need to – we do not want to go one more mile with this guy. This gives us an easy out. We aren't sure where our driver's journey is going to end up but it might not be Santa Rosa. So we tell him, "No thanks. We'll take a pass. We'll stay here and catch a ride later."

He's surprised and a bit put off, but he says, "Okay, see you later." And off he goes.

At sunrise we awaken, two dumb college students with our camp gear in Eastern Wyoming. We feel pretty happy to be there, but if you've ever been to that part of the country in the summer, you know that sometimes the wind blows all day, strong and steady. Big wind, with tumbleweeds flying by. From a car it can just seem boring, but when you're out there walking, it's tough.

But we grit our teeth and hike out of there, and soon get a string of short local rides. This is Tom Joad country, a great place to experience but young cowboys in pickup trucks would sometimes fuck around with you, try to scare you, confuse you, threaten you, maybe beat you up. We have long hair so we're prime targets, as we would learn.

Short-hop rides can be interesting too – we get one from a guy in one of those stand-up delivery trucks, where he had to stand up to drive. He takes us about four miles. Then a girl in a muscle car with an eight-track blasting, ten more miles or so. You can do that all day and never get across Wyoming. But then, we get picked up by this family hop-scotching their way across the state along Route 80 to visit various extended family. Amazingly, they stop and pick us up – two random long-hair guys by the side of the road – even though they already have a bunch of people in the car. They open the trunk for us to stash our packs and we ride in the back seat crammed in with two other people, with four more jammed in up front. Throughout that day, they drop us off, stop in on some relatives, then pick us up an hour or so later, three times! We don't catch many rides but theirs. They finally say to us, "Look, normally we don't pick up hitchhikers. But in your case we're making an exception, cuz you have long hair and around here, a sheriff can pick you up and either beat the shit out of you or throw you in jail. So we're doing you a favor."

We say, "Thanks, we appreciate it."

People would take responsibility in that way. Here are two total strangers, looking young and kind of lost. They're going to get in trouble unless we take care of this situation.

And so there you go – the milk of human kindness does flow.

After all those rides, we get stuck for a long time in a town called Wamsutter, a place I hope to never get stuck in again. By now it's late afternoon, with a hot dusty wind. We're on the side of the road and a maroon pickup truck comes barreling along, a big tank mounted on brackets right behind the cab for fueling up tractors and farm vehicles. The driver pulls over. There are already some people in the pickup, the cab is full and there's one other guy already in back, plus the big gas tank. We jump in the back, not much conversation at that point, and we take off.

The crew is friendly but moving fast and with a fugitive sense. I have no idea how much of what they're telling us is true, but if true they're on a bit of a crime spree. They do have weed and we get stoned with them up in the cab, which makes the whole thing even weirder. They aren't particularly menacing or anything to us, but tell tales of ongoing criminal adventure that I half-believe. Then they say, "We're gonna stop and find a grocery store." So we find one and on the way in they say to me, "You go buy something." So I buy a candy bar and some gum, chatting with the clerk while they're working the aisles and stuffing food in their pants. I pay for my candy and we all file out the door. The clerks are either too nervous to do anything or too dumb to notice and we get out of there with no problem. So then they say, "Well, now we need some gas." We offer to pitch in a small amount, but it's not enough to get that beast very far.

The tank in the back is a fifty-gallon reserve tank and they're going to fill it up. We stop next to a railroad maintenance truck parked on the side of the road, planning to siphon its gas into our tank, but they can't get the siphon hose to draw. So we pile back in and go a little farther down the road where we find a small mining yard with a gas pump out in the lot. So they pull over to the gas pump, pull out a crowbar, and pry the lock off. They get it flowing and it takes us about ten nervous minutes to fill up the reserve tank.

So now we've got enough gas to go a long way. Barry and I are in back again, looking at each other saying, "What's our choice?" In the middle of the night in Western Wyoming, it's getting colder and either we're going to keep riding with these criminals or get out and have no ride. So we're going to stick it out for awhile.

We reach the outskirts of Salt Lake City and they lean out the window and say, "Are you guys cold back there?" In the mountains, even in summer, it gets cold at night in an open truck pickup truck bed. We're shivering in our sleeping bags. They decide, we've gotta

find a cap for the back of the pickup so these
hitchhikers don't freeze. So they drive down
into Salt Lake and pull up at a place that sells
truck caps, and there's a whole yard full of
them behind a tall chain-link fence. They pile
out of the cab and climb the fence, and they're
quickly in there scouting for the right-sized cap.
Barry and I are sitting in the back of the truck
thinking, should we leave? But how can we,
when they're on a criminal mission of mercy
for us?

It'll be a lot warmer in here with a cap in place.
But if they're caught we're probably going
to jail with them. We'd surely give it the old
college try – "Oh, but officers we're just college
students, we didn't know what was going
on!" But we do know so I don't know how
convincing we'd be.

All of a sudden we see them sprinting out
of the dark yard and one yells, "The night
watchman saw us!" They scamper up over the
fence and jump back into the truck and boom,
we're back on the road. No cap but no cops,
so we're good. The rest of the night we sit up
getting stoned and talking with them about

prison, rotating between the warm cab and the cold truck bed.

Later we reach the outskirts of Reno and my friend and I are sitting in the back again, watching the traffic behind us. I watch a police car turn to follow us, then its lights revolving. Just like that we're pulled over.

Barry and I are huddled in the back as the cop walks up, ignoring us and focusing on the guys up front. Earlier, they'd been talking about going down into Reno to snatch purses. That was their next plan.

I look at my friend and we silently agree – this might be a good time to take our leave. We slowly shift our stuff over to the far side of the truck bed, then quietly slide and shimmy up over the side and walk away. Unlike Lot's wife, we do not look back, we just keep walking. And no one stops us. We walk all the way to the Reno bus station, where we buy tickets for San Francisco. Enough of this crime wave. Even the heroic Kerouac knew enough to just take a bus now and again.

So having hitchhiked that far west made me much more tolerant of making the return trip east on a bus for two and a half days, because as unpleasant as a bus can be, you always knew you're going to keep moving. And the bus was air conditioned. But after I buy the bus ticket I have $12 left and five or six days until the dorms open back at Kenyon. So to prepare for the trip, consciously or unconsciously imitating Kerouac, I spend a few bucks and make a sack of peanut butter sandwiches. I also have a bunch of homegrown joints I'd rolled, courtesy of friends in California.

From San Francisco to Cleveland I ride the hours and hop out at rest stops – half-hour breaks for the driver. I go off into the woods or bushes and lay down, eat a peanut butter sandwich, drink water, and smoke a joint. It made the hours much more interesting.

I remember sitting on the curb outside the bus station in Rock Springs, Wyoming having just smoked a joint at the far edge of the parking lot and some guys drive by in a pickup truck, call me a hippie and throw a firecracker at me. That was a highlight.

I finally get back to Cleveland and I don't have any money left. So I have to hitch the final hundred-or-so miles to Kenyon College, which seems the perfect ending to my saga. An easy string of short rides gets me there within a few hours and I feel like a pro at this.

Problem is, I'm now there with no there – the college doesn't allow early arrivals into the dorms and enforces that rule rigidly. I have my camping gear and decide to go ask a professor if I can camp in his backyard. Kindly and bravely he allows me to do so. I set up my tent and take out my tiny one-burner stove, getting settled in, and the professor and his wife keep coming out and saying, you know, you don't have to stay outside, you can come in and stay with us! "Oh no," I say, "truly, I don't want to impose – I'll just camp in the yard." And now I realize their neighbors might have been asking them, why are you making that kid sleep out in your yard?

But I felt I was being a good guy in that way, and in any event their Gambier backyard was luxury compared to lying in a ditch. The next day the professor must have talked to someone in charge because they call me in and say, we heard you were back, and we need volunteers for freshman orientation – we'll let you into your dorm room today, but we'll be giving you work to do. I say, "Fine, I'll do it!" So I have my room and can actually eat in the dining hall, which is great, because I otherwise have no food and no money.

Greek Gangster, Gay Savior

Even a star-crossed hitch-hiking trip can get you where you're going, if not by the planned route.

I'm a student at McGill University in Montreal in 1973. In early February I decide to take a long weekend break from studies and see some friends in central New York state in a college town called Oneonta in the Catskill Mountains. To get there I have to hitch across the U.S. border and down the Adirondack Northway through the High Peaks Wilderness, about a 4-hour drive straight through, but in hitchhiking time more like 6-8 if I'm lucky. The Northway has long desolate stretches through the Adirondack wilderness. My hope is to be blessed with a long ride that carries me through an easy winter hitch. It's been known to happen.

Crack of dawn, I'm out the door of my apartment on Av du Parc, stopping to get a fresh-baked bagel from the St-Viateur Bagel Shop, in the basement where two older Jewish men tend to boiling and baking the best bagels known to man. Sesame or poppy, that's it. You grab a couple from a hot basketful.

I'm walking a good pace down Parc past McGill and on through downtown, to René Lévesque Boulevard, where an entrance for the A15 South leads straight to Blackpool, Quebec where U.S. Customs and Border Protection has a large border station.

As I stand there shivering at the A15 I'm soon graced with an early gift – a trucker pulls over. I climb up into the cab and thank him, asking how far he's going. He says, "I'm going all the way to Charleston South Carolina but I can't take you across the border. I'm going to have to let you off before we cross. If you were carrying drugs or something, I could get in trouble."

"Okay," I say, "that's fine – I appreciate the ride."

"Where you headed?" he asks.

I tell him central New York, a town in the Catskills called Oneonta. To see some friends.

When we reach the border, he pulls over to the right and brakes to a gradual stop. I thank him again and climb down with my pack. So now as he pulls away I'm walking across a wide plaza leading to the lanes and booths where drivers stop to chat with U.S. Customs officers. Eternal optimist, I'm wondering if I might just walk on through and keep walking. To the extent there was a plan, that was it.

So I take that tack. But as I reach the booth, a uniformed sleeve reaches out to block me and a narrow face under a large hat asks me where I'm going.

I point ahead, down the road – "New York."

"You're walking?" he says, eyebrows up to the brim.

I shrug.

He motions over his shoulder with his thumb, *"Inside!"*

So I stroll inside and approach the counter where two desk officers are watching. They look me over and one says, "What's your story?"

So I say, "They told me to come inside?"

The other one gestures for my backpack, which I place up on the counter. He gives it a very cursory search then pushes it back to me. The first one wants to know where I think I'm going and informs me that hitchhiking is illegal and they do not allow it here. I'll have to wait for the bus.

So I ask him, "When does the bus get here?"

"Between three and four this afternoon," he says.

It's a gut punch – here it is a little past nine in the morning and now I'll have to kill an entire hitchhiking day waiting for a bus that I'll have to pay for? If I could afford a bus I'd have taken one.

"Sit over there," they say, pointing to a row of theater seats bolted to the wall. Crestfallen – crushed – I sulk on over feeling totally thwarted, my glory trip skidding to a hard stop as I plop into the seat. I sit there fuming for a half hour. I'm also a bit paranoid, wondering whether I should make a trip to the restroom and flush away the single skinny joint I have hidden in my sock. I'm thinking if these guys get bored, they may decide to do a more thorough search of my pack and person. I've heard some stories.

As I'm weighing this out – on the other hand, it might be nice to have that joint later, could be a long day – I see out the window the nearest lane has an officer pulling over a large black car, waving the driver out so they can search it. The driver, a swarthy fellow with slick black hair in a sharkskin suit, is arguing from the moment he exits the car. I can't hear them but can read in the body drama his ire at being thus detained. He's waving his arms. The officers wave him into the desk officers and he comes charging through the double door like an angry bull.

"You got no right! I'm a taxpayer! I'm a citizen!"

The desk officers listen, blank-faced. "Sit over there," they say to him, pointing over to me. But he's relentless, arguing. Finally they command him, "Take a seat!" He marches over, seething.

Now he sidebars his angry laments to me as we sit beside each other – "got no right!" And I'm nodding and sharing anger in kind – "they're making me wait all day for a damn bus," I say. He grunts and continues fuming, fully aggrieved.

When he takes a breath, I ask him – "Tell me, how far are you going when they let you go?"

"Baltimore," he says flatly.

"I tell you what," I say, "I'm trying to get to Albany New York, it's right on the way, down by the New York Thruway. Can you give me a ride?"

He glances at me with a sour expression and does not respond, goes back to griping under his breath and looking at his watch.

Now I'm looking over at the desk officers and I see two men in suits emerge from the back room. They must have come in a back way. They've got papers in their hands. The desk officers are looking over and pointing us out. The suits approach. My new Baltimore friend revs up again.

They cut him off quick, flashing government IDs, asking if he is Nico Alexopoulos. He acknowledges that he is. I'd thought maybe Italian, but he's Greek.

The suits serve him with a subpoena to appear in Federal Court in Baltimore on such-and-such date regarding an investigation into the disappearance of a labor union official that occurred about the same time Nico left the country, more than a month ago. His family is in the construction business.

He snatches the subpoena from the agent's hand and sarcastically asks if he's free to go now?

They answer, "Show up in court Nico or we'll come get you."

He lurches off toward the double door, cursing over and under his breath, and I grab my backpack. He blows through the door and I'm close behind. When he reaches his car he sees me in the windshield reflection and turns to me saying, "What the hell are you doing?"

I say, "Albany?"

He gives me a pained look then shakes his head and growls, *"Get in the car!"*

I jump in, setting my backpack at my feet. He slams the door, hopping mad now, and peels out of the Customs area with wailing rubber and smoke. He rockets south on the New York State Northway, diving back into his rampaging soliloquy about they got no right. I try to settle in, exuberant that my travel day may be recovered, though I've lost a couple precious hours.

I'm thinking, by the time we get to Albany it'll be afternoon; it gets dark early here, wintertime. I should have him take me to Kingston, forty minutes past Albany; the route from there to Oneonta is better traveled than the one that cuts over from Albany. I'm heading through some hinterlands, could get stranded.

As he fusses and fumes, I'm feeling like I don't want to listen anymore and try feigning sleep but he doesn't shut up. I wonder if maybe a hit or two off the number hidden in my sock might mellow him out and make the ride more enjoyable. But as I'm reaching down to retrieve it his rant takes a sudden right turn and now he's saying they (the border officers) should be "leaving taxpayers like me alone and going after the goddam drug people, those bum bastards!" And so my arm withdraws, leaving the joint where it hides for maybe later.

Miles go by. After a quiet pause I ask him,
"Could you take me a little past Albany, to
Kingston? The hitching is better there."

He snorts, shakes his head and says, "You said
Albany."

"Oh," I say, "I really appreciate the ride, and
Kingston's just another half-hour or so."

"Albany" he says.

And not another word until he skids to a stop
at the first Albany exit.

So now I'm standing roadside and it's gray and
snowing lightly as an invisible sun gets low.
It's cold and I'm dressed for it, but I begin to
wonder whether I should just hitch over to
the nearby university and find a place there to
crash for the night. It's another couple or few or
many hours to Oneonta. Hitchhiking at night
on Route 23, you're basically out in the woods
on a little ribbon of asphalt and it's winter and
it's cold and it's snowing. I could make an early
start tomorrow in daylight.

But no. I want to be there tonight. I decide to keep going. I walk down off the highway shoulder and toward a county road branching off to the lower Catskill Mountains. By the time I reach the county road the snowfall is thickening. And with a few short hops taking me nowhere fast, I'm mostly walking, trudging, trying to shrug off uncertainty.

A couple of short rides, a couple miles, a few miles, a few more miles. I'm making a little progress, but not rapid progress. And so I'm near the town of Guilderland and the road is quiet, not much moving. A few cars pass but not many, and nobody's stopping.

Someone brakes as they pass me, a small coupe. Given the circumstances, I just jump in the car. Normally, you go to the driver's side window first, you don't just jump in. You talk to them, all friendly-like – how far are you going? Just to get a read on the situation. I haven't turned down many rides in my life, but I've turned down a few. If a driver is drunk and I can smell it and see it, if he's got a gang of guys in the car, yeah, I'm not getting in there.

But when circumstances are dire you just jump in the car. So I do, to a friendly greet from a young driver Evan, turning his hand out for a shake, chatty and friendly. We hit it right off as the snow thickens like a plot.

Unlike my gangster friend Nico, Evan is a talker but with tone and spirit that are bright, upbeat, funny, and eager to chat. I'm telling him about leaving Montreal this morning, the trucker, customs, the gangster, the Feds or whoever they were, and the snow keeps falling. And as his questions keep me talking I realize I feel this sensation on my left thigh. I look down and see his pinky. He's cat-stroking my left leg.

Great, I think – the remains of a long jagged day. I'm feeling tired, hungry and jagged and in no mood for romance. So I say, "All right, pull over."

And he says, "What?" and pulls his hand away.

I say, "Pull the car over and stop, I'm getting out."

He says "Oh no, it's okay."

So I get angry, draw my right arm up and bark at him, "Pull the car over or I'm gonna punch you in the head!"

Evan jerks the steering wheel, slides to a stop on the snowy shoulder and bursts into tears.

I'm one foot out the door and he's sitting there with his head on the wheel, sobbing. And so I stop and say to him, "Listen, I'm not really going to hit you. I'm not going to do anything, but I'm straight. I don't want to do anything with you."

And he's sobbing and sniffling, saying "I'm only going ten miles or so. I didn't mean to... I just need some company."

So I stay in the car. He gets it back on the road and now he's talking about his life, his day to day. He's so lonely. He owns a flower shop in a small town near here. "There's no one like me around," he says. Like almost all queer people then, he's closeted and careful. I have friends like him – college pals, professors – living under this regime of prohibition. Nothing easy about it.

I say, "Look, I'm sympathetic, and sorry I acted like a lunatic back there – I have friends like you who I respect, but they also respect me. I'm just wired straight. I like girls. And as long as the respect goes both ways, I'm fine."

He's clearly grateful just to be able to talk openly with someone. The tension is gone and now he's talking about flowers and boys.

And so I'm thinking, this is what he does. He goes out and cruises and on the rare night there's someone hitchhiking. So random and difficult! And completely human.

We're approaching the point where he's about to turn off. And he says to me, "Have you eaten anything today?"

"I ate a bagel this morning when I was leaving Montreal," I tell him. "But no, not since then."

He says, "You must be starving. Look, there's a road house up ahead where I turn off, near my shop – let's stop and get something to eat there. I'll be happy to buy us dinner. The food is good and it's a laid-back place, they know me."

The prospect of hot food is very tempting. I say "Sure, that sounds great. I'd appreciate that." So we stop and go into this roadside bar. I order a burger and water, he gets a salad and a beer. We sit and talk for a good while. I feel sympathy for him within the limits of my own understanding and my own sexual inclinations. I think I understand his situation a little better, and he mine.

We finish our meal and walk outside. It's snowing pretty hard. And he says to me, "How much further?"

"I don't know, probably another forty or so miles, something like that."

He says "Well, I'm not going to put you out on the road on a night like this. My place is right down that road over there. You can stay the night and get a start in the morning."

"No," I say, "I'm not going to your house. I'm heading on."

He pauses then says, "Okay. Then I'm driving you to Oneonta."

"No way," I say. "You've done enough for me."

"No way is right," he says. "No way I'm letting you out hitchhiking in this. *Get in the car.*"

I laugh. "You're the second person to tell me that today," I say. "But you said it nicer."

We get in the car and we head out again, slow going. Plows are out pushing the heavy snow around, we pass a number of them on the way as we talk. With a meal in my belly and feeling warm, I'm grateful for every one of these hard miles taken in comfort and good company.

We finally reach Oneonta. He pulls up in front of my friends' house and now it's late, well after midnight, and I thank him for his kindnesses and hug him hard. I jump out with my backpack and just like that our lives diverge. Evan wheels the car around and heads back homeward, more hours of driving ahead on wicked roads, having saved me this night.

I turn around. The house is dark. I expected my friends would be up, but I knock on the door and there's no answer. So I think they must be

out at the bars. I consider going off looking
for them but Oneonta has almost fifty bars and
who knows where they're hanging. Anyway I'm
really tired and their house has a covered porch
with a chair, so I slump down to wait for them.
I'm warm enough to be comfortable, sitting
here watching it snow. The town is quiet, roads
are soft. Incredibly peaceful and wonderful to
be, finally, here.

This exhausted joy of arrival reminds me, oh
yeah, I've got that joint in my sock. So I reach
down, carefully pull it out and straighten it, light
it and take a poke. I sit there with a rounding
sense of serenity – the world and human waves
crashing thereupon having delivered me unto
this place. A long day rich with road glamour.

And in that blissful state, I fall asleep.

It turns out my friends are not out. I awaken
just before dawn. The winter sky is a fuzzy
dark gray, orange glimmers beginning to show.
The snow has ceased and the air is still, an early
quiet, things just beginning to stir. I hear a car
off in the distance and then a truck.

I rise off the achy chair and peer through the front door window to see one of my buddies in the kitchen in his pajamas and slippers, making coffee. I knock on the window, startling him. He blinks at the sight of me, tilts his head like dogs do, then quickly shuffles over and opens the door.

"What are you doing here?" he says. "I thought you were in Canada?"

I say, "I was in Canada this time yesterday morning. I hitchhiked down."

He says, "You've been hitching all night?"

"No, I've been sleeping on your front porch all night. I knocked on the door and nobody answered, so I figured you guys were out. I fell asleep in that chair waiting for you to come home and I just woke up."

He smiles, bemused, scratches his head and says, "You want some coffee?"

Boy, do I.

Stolen Feast

One significant advantage of youth over older age lies in the ability to withstand discomfort and not notice it as much as one might thirty, forty, or fifty years on. One of those discomforts common to hitchhikers is hunger – you may not have the foresight or the wherewithal to pack along an adequate amount of food. If the rides don't come so easily and you wind up stranded in a remote place, you might not have anything to eat for a stretch. You might not have money to buy it, even if it's available. On many occasions I would set out hitchhiking with very little money and no food, but it's rarely a huge concern for me because I'm young and durable. Eventually I'll land in a place where there's food to eat.

On this particular trip, I'm trying to get from Boulder, Colorado back to New York after attending a writer's conference as a young devotee of the Black Mountain writers and Beat poets. A gang of them held forth at this writer's event at the university in Boulder, which a year later, in 1974, evolved into the Naropa Institute and the Jack Kerouac School

of Disembodied Poetics under the tutelage
of poets Anne Waldman and Allen Ginsberg,
among others. At the conference I managed to
connect with one of my heroes, poet Robert
Creeley, who gave me a bit of his time there
in Boulder and entré to his undergrad and
graduate classes at SUNY Buffalo and his spare
guest room at 400 Fargo on Buffalo's west side.

But first, I have to get back to New York. I've
spent every dime I had at the conference,
now facing a several day hitch to get back east
– no money, no food. I knew this would be
challenging. As a skinny kid I had few reserves
to draw upon. I wonder, how best to do this?

So I take a step I'd not taken before nor since.
Desperate times, desperate measures. I'm
marching through Boulder on my way out
of town, looking for a highway to take me
towards Denver. I pass an Italian restaurant,
then step back to gaze in the window and read
the posted menu. It all looks very, very good.
The restaurant is empty, past the lunch rush
and before the dinner rush, but it's open. So
I walk around the corner, stash my rucksack
behind a dumpster, duck into a gas station

restroom to freshen up and comb my hair, then enter the restaurant.

There is no one in the dining room when I walk in. I wait a minute or so, looking around, noting the restroom right up there by the front door. I walk back to the swinging doors of the kitchen and look in. A server is having his lunch at the prep counter. He looks up, says he's sorry, didn't know you were here, and follows me back into the dining room to seat me at a table. With the menu spread open in front of me I proceed to order a feast: soup, appetizer, salad, pasta and meatballs, and dessert. Over the next forty minutes I eat everything he brings me, wolfing it all down while the server and a cook hang out in the kitchen.

When I'm done, I sit back and take a deep breath. My guy has disappeared again into the kitchen, where I can barely hear him chit-chatting with the cook. I get up very quietly from the table, peek in the kitchen and see they are occupied, so I tip-toe for the front door. At the restroom, I take one last glance back, then open the door quietly and slide out like a fat snake. Moving quickly, I retrieve my pack and walk a block, then make a right and walk down a side street to stay off the main drag, where I fear I'll be pinched by a passing cop if the restaurant guys have phoned in the crime of the century. As I think it through, I figure they haven't – they know a hungry hippie when they see one. I circle back to the main road, stick my thumb out and quickly snag a ride toward Denver.

I've thought back with some regret to that act of thievery. But I knew I needed one meal in my gut before starting a journey of several days. Since then I've tried to offload some of the bad karma by being kind to strangers, giving rides to hitchhikers, and buying food for people needing some. I've also sent blessings to that kindly server who I reckon might have had a clue about what I was up to. He provisioned me for a long trip homeward.

Gothenburg, Nebraska

A series of short hops gets me from Boulder
down to Denver, routes 93 to 36. I'm walking
along occasionally sticking out my thumb,
but nothing's happening. I reach a large gas
station where I watch a fellow drive up in a big
ferocious-looking Plymouth Fury and pull in to
a gas pump.

I'm walking over to his car as he gets out. I say
to him "Hi, I'm hitching east, are you headed
that way?" He's in his mid-thirties, tall, grizzled-
looking, what you might maybe call ruggedly
handsome. Bill is his name, we shake hands.

Looking me over he says "I'm going to
Baltimore, but first I gotta go to Gothenburg
Nebraska to see a lady." I say "Well, you want
some company?" and he says "Sure, okay." I
throw my bag in the car and wait for him to
finish gassing up before I hop in.

When he gets behind the wheel I think, I better
clear this first. I say, "There's only one thing. I'd
like to help out with gas money but I don't have
any money." He says "Don't worry about it."

As he's saying this, a kid who works at the gas station saunters over. "Hey Mister," he says, "you look at your tires lately?"

Bill looks at him and doesn't say anything. The kid continues.

"Those tires are bald. I wouldn't drive across the street on those tires."

Bill just shrugs. And off we go.

I can see right away he's a little heavy on the gas as we lurch towards the interstate. I say to him "So you're going all the way to Baltimore? That's great!"

He says "Yeah. I'm a Merchant Marine." He leans back in his seat and says, "I got to go pick up my car."

And I say, "What are you going to do with this car?" He says "I don't know. Sell it. Junk it. I got a better car in Baltimore."

I ask him how long he's been out at sea.

He says "I've been out almost a year. Africa, Middle East, around to South Asia. I wound up shipping into Oakland. So, I just picked up this junker to drive across to Baltimore to get my good car."

I say to him, "You're a Merchant Marine! How's that life?"

Bill shrugs and says, "It's a living. I'm seeing the world and getting paid."

I say, "How's the world looking these days?"

He gives me a side eye and says, "Not all good."

We cruise along for a while in silence and then he says to me, "We're going to take a little detour. I've got to go up to Gothenburg."

I say, "To see your girlfriend?"

He looks at me and says, "She's a hooker, she ain't my girlfriend."

We're on the interstate now, booming along. Bill likes to drive about 90. As I sit beside

him reading poetry, I listen to the front tires
bouncing off the road in a syncopated rhythm. I
think about what the kid at the gas station said
about the tires being bald. I figure at 90 miles an
hour, a blowout will probably be pretty exciting.
The car has no seat belts. I decide not think too
much more about that.

Bill isn't terribly talkative. He seems lost in
the long view. I occasionally nudge him into
conversation, but it's always brief, so I spend
quality time reading Creeley and looking out
the window and not thinking about those
tires. When we get to Gothenburg I see a
storybook Midwestern Main Street – a big,
broad-shouldered boulevard, shop-lined, mostly
deserted. Bill pulls up in front of this ancient
hotel with the front door kind of flapping
in the breeze like in an old western. He gets
out without saying anything to me, grabs a
small bag from the back seat and heads in. I'm
thinking, how do I handle this – I have no
money but Bill told me we'd be staying here
for the night. He hadn't offered to pay for my
room and I have no money to pay for it, but
I think maybe we might negotiate that at the
front desk.

So I follow him in. He's standing at a front desk that isn't really a desk, it's just a small window above a small counter hung on the wall. Bill's not happy. "What's this joker doing?" he says. "Come on!"

He's standing there ringing the bell and getting no response. So I join him, stand with my backpack and wait. Nobody shows up in response to the bell, so Bill sticks his head into the service window and calls out, gets no response there either. "To hell with this this," he says, "I'm going upstairs to grab a room. We can check in later," and off he goes up the stairs.

I follow him up to a worn hallway lined with rooms, all doors hanging open. He goes in one room and I go in another. Mine is of generous size with shabby, faded wallpaper, a worn coverlet on the bed, one of those squeaky old metal frame beds with a metal headboard. But also a gigantic window facing out onto Main Street, with long slender chintz curtains billowing on the breeze.

I hear Bill close his door and go back down the stairs, heading out to find his friend I suppose.

I have nowhere to go, no money to spend, so I just lie down on the bed to read awhile. I'm soon drunk on the smell of alfalfa, the breeze making ballet curls of the chintz curtains, a penetrating aroma of earth and grass. It's soon dark and I put down my book, turn in and fall asleep, hungry but happy in my dreams.

When I wake up in the morning, Bill is pounding on my door. There's a small sink in the room, I splash some water on my face, grab my backpack, stumble downstairs and get in the car, half-awake. He joins me a minute later, revs up the car, squeals the tires and we're off.

We get a little ways out of town and he looks at me and says, "Did you pay for your room?"

"No. Did you pay for yours?"

He says "Yeah, I paid for mine. I left money on the counter."

"Well, I don't have any money. I told you that."

He snorts and says, "How are you going to eat between here and Baltimore?"

I say, "I'm not."

He shrugs and punches the gas, takes us back up to 90 or 95 miles an hour. We syncopate eastward, bald tires singing like a barbershop quartet.

We make fast progress, Bill not backing off even a little. He takes me all the way to Harrisburg, where he can shoot straight south to Baltimore and I can hitchhike north through Pottsville, Pittston and Scranton, straight up to Binghamton and on over to Oneonta, homeward bound.

Creeley

Bob Creeley's offer to let me sit in on his
classes at Buffalo is the golden payoff of that
trip, which began when I saw an ad in a literary
journal for a writer's conference in Boulder,
earlier that summer. I'd just fallen into Charles
Olson's work, absorbed by its reaches, a strong
voice pushing postmodern poetics. I know
that he and Creeley shared a long working
relationship and want to know more about that.

I'm working my way through college and
spending little on anything else, tuition about all
I can muster in young earnings. That summer
I'm working at the college ski hill with a crew
of juvenile delinquents and a 1940s-era Willys
jeep. Four of us pile on and that little beast
climbs every hill. We clear trails, haul brush, and
hand-dig drainage ditches with pickaxes.

The writer's conference is near summer's end,
when I can take off for a week or so. Lacking
cash for transit, I'm looking at several days
hitch to get there and several days back. A
professor friend provides a solution – several of
the English faculty chip in and buy me one-

way airfare to Denver. Incredibly kind and thoughtful of them! We have a good laugh in the hallway outside their offices – "One way means one way," they say.

"I'm not allowed to come back?"

They laugh. Even now, I smile at the thought of my younger-brother fellowhood with those young professors, me looking up and outward.

So they get me there, and a marvelous time I have until the long road home. I want to get some time with Creeley but every time I try he's swarmed by twenty others. Then on the last night of the conference he delivers a reading to a packed hall, and in hearing him perform his work I suddenly get it. I hear what he's doing and its resonance with Olson's work. He wows the crowd such that, at the end, when he puts down the mic and walks off, there's this moment when the audience is just knocked out, a beat and a half of stunned silence, then long, clamorous applause.

The next day I walk over to conference HQ to say goodbye to folks and there's Bob, and the

two of us finally get a chance to talk. I tell him
of my interest in Olson's *Maximus Poems* but
also the *Black Mountain Review,* which Bob had
published on Mallorca in the 1950s when I was
a toddler.

He has such easy grace as we chat. He asks
where I'm living and I tell him Oneonta, in the
Catskills. He says he's teaching an undergrad
class at Buffalo on Wednesday afternoons and a
graduate seminar Thursday mornings, "you're
welcome to join us anytime. Whenever you can
make it."

So with pockets otherwise empty, that's the
gold I carry back home.

Then as luck has it, the road gets easier. Back
home, I'm planning to hitch to Buffalo weekly,
or as often as I possibly can, when a friend
offers his car, says he can easily do without it a
couple days a week. So there it is.

The car is an Opel Cadet wagon. It's aged,
rusty and rickety, but it runs. Its owner drives
with his window down and his left arm braced
on the doorframe, even in bitter winter cold,

trusting more in the strength of the doorframe than in the floorboards below his seat. He fears falling through and dragging ass on pavement. I find the car to be trusty, good on gas and far more reliable than hitching. I drive over early Wednesdays, catch Bob's afternoon class, then sleep in the Opel and sit in with the Thursday morning grad group before driving home.

I'm having coffee with one of the grad students on a Thursday morning when he asks me where I'm staying on my weekly visits. "In the car," I tell him.

"Oh man," he says, "this is Buffalo – it's gonna be very cold here soon." I tell him it's okay, I have an arctic sleeping bag on loan from the college ski lodge.

He says, "I'd invite you to stay with us but we just had a baby. My wife will kill me if I bring someone home now."

"Don't worry," I tell him, "I'll be fine!"

So I guess he spoke to Creeley that week, because the next time I show up Bob takes me aside and says, "You're sleeping in your car? This is Buffalo, man! Do you know what's coming? Fierce winter! Tell you what, we have a spare bedroom and my wife Bobbie is in Bolinas. You come stay at our place, glad to have you."

So I do. He's living above a little grocery store over on Fargo, in west Buffalo. I walk up the stairs with him for the first time to find this lovely apartment with a settled grace, humble and rich, simple and orderly.

"Wow, your place is neat," I marvel.

"I like the articulation of clean surfaces," he says.

That stays with me, all this time.

We sit at night and talk at his kitchen table, smoking joints and cigarettes, drinking tea, reading poems. A Rauschenberg white painting lords over the small kitchen, which holds artifacts and made things from a host of old friends. In fact, the entire apartment does. Everywhere I look I find keen objects to examine, read, and hold in my hands.

Most weeks we eat soul food at a local bar then retire to 400 Fargo to relax and visit. A string of soulful Wednesday nights, his patience with my nineteen year old eager talk so comforting and disarming. With little experiential intelligence of my own, I was a keen listener. His rhythms of thought are a pacing, a wobbling walk with steady eye. He edits as he speaks, and freely. And as it is, he makes sense to me. He is a constant builder. I hear his measures.

Once the semester is complete he heads out west again, and from there, outward. I keep in touch and when he's back in Buffalo I see him again, and then he comes to Oneonta, where we've lined up a reading. Creeley draws well, a known name, a remarkably well-selling serious poet of all things, not in the greeting card business exactly. We hang out at a college bar but he doesn't drink anymore, god bless him. I think the younger, drunken Bob was not always such a good guy. I think he changed when he gave up alcohol for better things, and became not just a better man but one of the more generous human souls to ever walk the planet. Brilliant, as the Irish say. You feel you've been shined.

An outpouring of grief when Bob dies in 2008. The following evening, jazz vocalist Kurt Elling pauses his song *Man In The Air* to perform Creeley's poem *The Signboard* at NYC's Rose Hall, in elegant tribute.

The word you keep hearing is generous. Such a rough, kind and gracious man, such a thoughtful human. With work always in hand.

My experiences in my hitching years were elevated by his measures. He shared a sharp, ranging focus, fashioning poetic form by living it, breathing it, and inviting you in.

Oklahoma City Weed

My hitchhiking days overlap with some truck driving days – I took a job driving straight rigs loaded with semi-precious artwork to art auctions nationwide. Most of my runs were three-city tours where I'd rendezvous with TV actor auctioneers conducting fundraiser art showings and auctions with charitable groups and Rotarians and PTAs. Other runs were straight NY to LA, transferring art between the company's east and west coast galleries and warehouses.

In those couple of years it's rare that I head off on a three-city truck-driving run, or a coast-to-coast, without bringing a little stash of weed. Highway hours, I think at the time, should be just that – not way high but a little high. Most marijuana was way less powerful back then.

Absent our modern day cornucopia of audio media, entertainment is AM radio all the way – fading in and out, rolling like ethereal hillsides, waves of evangelizing, sales pitch, the odd music. Every now and then you find a gem, especially nighttimes – a jammering roadhouse with eager jazz and earnest blues filling the truck's cabin and illuminating the dark highway with glittering song, accompanied by some preaching.

But more often, your thoughts are the music.

Due to some missed connection or glitch of timing, I set off from NY for the west coast empty handed, no hooch to be had. The route westward offers opportunities to explore some back-city streets – in Nashville, Memphis, Little Rock – but I come up dry every time. It's beginning to feel jinxy, as if some sort of hex oil has been rubbed on my tires. Just as I resign to cruising the rest of the way without weed, I pull into a gas station in downtown Oklahoma City to fuel up and get some local directions. I'm looking for a certain Best Western hotel, near the state capitol.

First guy I see at the gas station is a black fellow strolling back towards his car. When I ask he provides careful directions, pointing me further downtown with a right and a left and a left and a right. I thank him and begin to turn away and this gas station angel says to me, "Hey – you get high?"

As I take his measure I feel the earth turn, a mesmerizing development straight out of hippie karma-land, Woo-woo-ville.

I smile and reply, "I do indeed. You got?"

"You can have a lid for ten," he says.

Bingo.

"I stopped in three cities on the way here and found nothing," I tell him. "I guess it's not 'til you stop looking that you find." And he laughs.

We complete our transaction standing beside his car. I take my sandwich bag stuffed with Mexican cannabis and off I go, gassed up and fully loaded.

His directions are wonderfully accurate. As I roll into the Capitol Best Western I see its parking lot is bustling with business-suited revelers. I'm told at the desk that it's the final day of the legislative session; clearly, the state legislators are ready to party with a rebel vengeance. I take a second floor room overlooking the pool, roll a fat one, and sit watching the elected portion of the state government devolve into a drunken poolside riot with suited men throwing panty-hosed women and each other into the deep end, patio furnishings soon to follow. Democracy at its energetic finest. And not bad weed, either.

Back to Bob

Takes me back to a story I'm told – the roots
of counterculture as tiny seeping wellsprings
percolating new ingredients into us all.

Bob is at Harvard but drinking a lot and
decides to enlist – it's 1944. The Army rejects
him because he's missing his left eye, lost as
a small boy to a car windshield. But he's able
to enlist with the American Field Service, a
US/British unit operating field hospitals and
ambulances in the India–Burma theater.

Months later, deep in a Burmese jungle, Bob
and his buddies are melting away. They've had
dysentery for weeks and now can barely eat.
Army rations make them ill, and any local food
is way too spicy for them. Dangerously hot, in
a very hot place. So they waste away, getting
skinnier by the day.

A local guy, an occasional fixer, shows up one
afternoon and says to them in his way,
"You must eat! You must eat! You will die!"

They tell him, we can't eat.

A green spark crosses his eye. "I know something to make you hungry," he says, and trots off into the jungle.

Soon he's back with a shoulder load of wild jungle cannabis. He shows them how to handle it, passes the pipe, turns them on.

Things shift, taking on new color and shine.

In fairly short order they do recover some appetite, holding steady by staying stoned, waiting for the war to end. It lends a smoother edge, a bit of the humor to a jungle situation.

Word finally comes war is over, they'll be evac'd soon. And then they wait and wait, weeks and more weeks, meanwhile refining their collection and processing skills, learning to work with leaf.

Now word comes that they're next up to ship out. Each man is allowed one backpack and one duffel bag, we'll truck you out, you'll be boarding a ship for the long ride home. They huddle, he and a buddy, deciding they can combine all their so-called personal effects into one duffel and fill the other with their best jungle weed.

So they do. Now they're aboard their transport, a large naval ship with broad open decks where crowds of returning troops camp out across the Pacific. There is absolutely no privacy but for rare moments when the latrine is empty. They camp nearby so they can duck in and blow a joint now and again.

Soon, back in Boston, Bob's in the jazz clubs getting to know the musicians. Late 1940s early counterculture begins to find its way, one beatnik poet at a time.

Paul's Hitch Home

Paul holds in his life's treasure chest the most
epic hitch story I've been told, because it alters
profoundly the route of his life, takes him beyond
roads to the end of a road, and to a decisive shift
in his brilliant lifetime on Earth.

This New York City boy drops out after a year of
college, finding it useless to him. The college is in
upstate New York and soon, Woodstock happens
nearby and he's there. His path becomes clear on
Yasgur's Farm – enough of college, I'm heading
west to learn from the real teachers.

Paul explores Arizona, takes pack mules out
into the desert and meets a Hopi medicine man
willing to teach him about nature's blessings, how
to gather, process, and use them. Later, he happens
into the Burro Race at Indian Days, a festival near
the Superstition Mountains, and with a pocketful
of Piñon nuts he connects with this wild burro,
they become brothers, and together they win
the race. Paul gets a $300 prize and the burro,
with the Forest Service rangers returning all the
others to the wild. He spends the next month
with Honcho, the burro, out in the Superstition

Mountains, Paul's supply of Piñon nuts and Peyote supplementing nature's food supply.

But then, needing to get back home to NYC, he returns the burro to the wild and heads out hitchhiking eastward. When he reaches western North Carolina he catches a ride with a van full of hippies and is telling them all about Arizona and Honcho and winning the Burro Race. He tells them about the Hopi shaman and the native medicines he's learned about.

One of his hosts interrupts.

"Man, you should check out southeast Ohio! That's where we're heading."

Paul says, "What's there?"

The guy explains, "The forests there, in Meigs County, have the most amazing understory load of native medicinal plants – Golden Seal, Black Cohosh, Slippery Elm, Witch Hazel – you can just wander through the woods and gather what you need. That whole biome has such abundance! One of the best places on earth for those medicinal species!"

Just as at Woodstock, decision sparks on the spot. Paul's not going back to NYC – he's heading to Meigs County, Ohio.

"I'm coming along with you guys if that's okay," he says. They're glad to have him along.

A condensed version of Paul's lifetime spent in Meigs County – more than fifty years later – includes developing Equinox Botanicals into a global provider of hand-made natural medicines developed in his FDA-certified apothecary. And field classes taught to graduate students on land Paul has restored by hand from abandoned strip-mined wreckage into clean, vibrant meadows, fields and streams. A lifetime of rich story made close to the Earth, most wonderfully told in his book, *The Big Herbs.*

Catching that ride in that particular van with those fellow hippies conveyed him forward to all of that. In Meigs County today, Paul Strauss is legend for his life lived and knowledge shared, working and walking the forest.

White Mike

No doubt about it – at the wrong place and time a hitch can get spooky and weird. Whether you're hitching or picking someone up you're sharing time and space with strangers.

Complete strangers can be completely strange.

And then there are incomplete strangers. Not every hitch begins roadside, there's also the kitchen table hitch (or the driveway or gas station hitch) whereby you make acquaintance with a person either needing or providing a ride and arrive at some agreement. Oh, you're heading to Omaha? I'm driving to Fort Collins Colorado tomorrow... It's face-to-face hitching with many advantages over the anonymous road shoulder, but can carry its own complications.

I meet White Mike across a kitchen table at a friend's house – a sort of communal flophouse ruled over by the first Hippie Mom in my direct experience. She lords over all joint-rolling from her kitchen table. She is the first mom I know who gets high with her sons, in league with the Blessed Weed since long before her sons were born. A mural of an hysterical Laughing Jesus dominates the wall behind her.

White Mike's name derives from his being the lightest-skinned kid in his public housing project in Fort Greene, Brooklyn back in the bad old days. Like almost all white people he's not really white but rather a shade of tan. He has some Native American blood for sure, I think when I meet him – or Meso-American, maybe Incan. Dark hair, parted in the middle; flat face; quick dark eyes. As the whitest kid in that 1960s housing project he had to step up his game to meet and beat the racial odds stacked against him. He did so by becoming the baddest-ass break-in artist around, the gutsiest little son-of-a-bitch of them all, the fastest runner with a near-magical ability to disappear in a blink. He specialized in burgling gun shops and as a teenager, sold handguns and rifles to Black Panthers in Bed Stuy. From an early age he wins respect, takes his beatings, and never meets a rule he won't break – totally fearless. With lightning instincts and liquid legs he evades arrest on many, many, but not all, occasions. For a time, he's incarcerated on Riker's Island, assigned to the Goon Squad, burying and exhuming bodies from the Potter's Field on that prison island. Years later, I'm startled but not surprised to see his grinning mug in a NYC tabloid. Arrested for trying to sell his baby son for drug money.

When I meet him, White Mike is a fugitive – on the lam again having jumped bail on a gun charge. He has a string of priors and stays in juvenile detention. But now he's over 21 and the stakes have risen accordingly. Local police are on the lookout for him with an All Points Bulletin throughout the New York metropolitan area.

At the time I'm driving trucks for an art gallery based in L.A., working from their New York warehouse. They keep me on the road near constantly for a year and a half, running truckloads of semi-precious artwork – limited edition prints, mainly – to charity art auctions all across the eastern U.S. The trucks are straight rigs and cutaway box vans so we aren't restricted to the Interstates, though we use them most of the time. I load up three catalogued shows and meet up with auctioneers in, say, Miami, Atlanta and Baton Rouge in one sweep. Then back to N.Y. to unload, reload, and back out again. They pay a decent salary plus per diem, all road expenses. I sleep in the truck some nights, and put the per diem cash to other purposes. Basically, I live on their dime in transit. I come back home for a night every couple weeks, drop a couple paychecks in the bank and head out again. My real destination is back to college with another year's tuition saved. This job gives me that along with some glorious rides and dubious people, including White Mike.

I agree to take him along to Florida, with scant thought of the level of illegality involved. It was simply, oh – you're fleeing prosecution? I'm driving a truck to Florida in the morning if you want a quick way out of town. Easy, when you're young and stupid as I was. A random act of kindness that could have led me directly to federal time, for someone I barely knew.

And to add to the planned excursion a longtime friend Rudy whom I'd promised to bring along on one of these trips calls in the chip – Florida? Great, he says. I figure, what the hell, we've got room for one more. Lots of company on this trip, given most of my runs are solitary.

Rudy meets up with us pre-dawn after White Mike steps out of some roadside bushes in thinning darkness near the casa de flop. Rudy is an aspiring writer, eventually an accomplished one, with a sweet innocence at that time. Rudy has a bit of Howdy Doodie in him.

So now we three head out in the truck with a load of art through New York City with Mike shielding his face or dropping his head to feign sleep whenever we roll through a toll booth. Rudy is very taken with Mike, fascinated in fact, and keeps addressing him as White Mike as if that might be the only acceptable form of address. Rudy comes from an educated family and privileged home – to him, Mike is an exotic. He's unaware of the fugitive scenario and seems not to notice Mike's occasional head duckings. He doesn't really know who he is with. I do, to a somewhat greater degree, but figure out pretty quickly that I can count on Mike only as long as luck holds out and not turn my back on him. He'll give me up in a moment to get away. He's deeper in his well than I care to follow, but I feel I can hold my own with him.

We roll for long hours with Rudy prodding
White Mike for more stories of growing up in
Fort Greene. At times Mike is obliging but then
he tires of the questions and waves Rudy off.
We make good time, I do all the driving. Mike
nods off awhile then awakens to tell me about
these girls he knows outside of Atlanta – pretty,
lots of fun – and we should call them. So we
push on for Atlanta hoping to hook up with
these girls.

As it turns out White Mike knows these girls
by virtue of having wrecked a stolen car with
them just a year earlier. Mike and his cousin
Jimmy were on a combined vacation and crime
spree in south Florida, made their way north
in a stolen car and picked up these girls outside
their school – they just rolled up and lay down
some jive, and these two daughters of prime
citizens get into the car with them and off they
all go. Soon there's was a police cruiser behind
them, and Jimmy stomps on the gas to flee and
manages to lose control and roll the car. They
all get thrown around but no one is badly hurt.
White Mike takes off running like he does, into
the mist, and somehow makes his way back
to Brooklyn. Jimmy is arrested, charged and

convicted, and sits in a Georgia prison. The girls are not charged; their parents are not amused.

I know bits and pieces of that but Rudy knows none of it. We take a room in a two-story strip motel on the Atlanta outskirts, relieved to finally get out of the truck. Right away Mike digs into the phone book for this girl's number. In the 1970s landline days that means dialing a house, a wall phone or desk phone, and whoever picks it up is who you talk to.

The girl's mother picks up.

Rather than hang up, White Mike soldiers on. Faking a southern drawl overlaying his thick Brooklyn brogue, he tells Mom he's a friend of Julie's "from school," and can he tawk to huh?

After a silent beat Mom says, "Julie isn't home. Is there a number where she can reach you?"

And Mike gives Mom the motel's phone number and our room number. More horny than crafty was he.

So now we sit and relax awhile in the shabby glory of our spacious room. Rudy lays back on one of the beds and opens a book while Mike flips on the TV. I'm fidgety after awhile and begin exploring – I open the door out onto the second-floor walkway overlooking the parking lot and stroll down its length, passing all the rooms. Once I reach the breezeway intersection I turn around and stroll back, stretching my legs after the long hours of driving.

A car slowly cruises into the parking lot, creeping along, then parks almost directly below me. From above I see a woman in the car, which seems hastily stuffed with piles of unfolded clothing, shoes, hangers, bedsheets and pillows.

The woman gets out of the car, looks up at me with a big smile and a wink and says, "Well hello there young man, would you kindly help me with my luggage?" Very flirty. She's maybe thirty years old, a bit disheveled, her hair in a rough bob. So I look back into the room at Mike, whose ears perk up, and I say to him "Hey, this chick wants help with her luggage." He grins, jumps up and joins me at the door and we head down the stairs.

When we approach the car she's on a harangue about her sorry-ass goddam husband and we see there is no luggage. We reach in and pull out handfuls of laundry and say to her, "This? You want this stuff up in your room?"

But she's already on her way to the stairs mid-monologue, "The sorry son of a bitch spends every dime we have and won't even, *Yes that's fine boys, follow me* his goddam boss is going to fire him, and my boss, don't even ask, is a useless buzzard who..." on and on as she strides up the stairs and unlocks a room three doors down from ours.

She walks in talking. We follow her with our armloads and she says "Put it over there," gesturing vaguely toward a corner. So we dump her stuff there, Mike and I looking at each other with confused grins, having not yet gotten in a word.

She continues the revolving rant against her goddam husband who won't leave and her damned boss who won't leave her alone and the unpaid bills she found, and steady as she goes her rant begins to bifurcate – split into two separate streams. She begins working in discrete comments out of context, such as: "If the bastard would just take out the damn garbage and make himself useless for a change *if you leave now, they'll let you go* can you believe it, last Christmas he didn't even *they're watching* he didn't even buy me a damn thing, the cheap creep *if I were you, I'd go, like, now* and then he wants to be all lovey-dovey, the horny bastard..." – all of this pouring out of her at a rapid pace with minor shifts of volume and inflection, her eyes shifting from fiery anger to side-eye slant along the way. The warning phrases are like pinches of salt she's adding to a hot stew, but we're frozen in place, neither of us saying a word, just speechless. Now Mike is giving me the side eye as if to say, let's get out of here. I nod and we bid her adieu with hasty thanks and goodbyes and a *"Good luck!"* from her.

Walking back towards our room we see a black unmarked sedan parked at the far side of the lot, directly across from us. Back in the room Ralph is engrossed in his book and Mike begins grabbing the few things he's brought, stuffing them into his little bag. Rudy looks up, puzzled.

"Did you help that woman –?" he begins, but Mike cuts him off – "Get your stuff, time to go."

"Go? We just got here. Where are we going?"

"Gone," says Mike, and heads for the door. He opens it just a crack, peering out across the parking lot at the black sedan, which does appear to have someone behind the wheel, and another someone beside him. Rudy jumps up, grabs his pack and book and is ready to go, although confused and uncertain of what gives here.

Mike and I huddle, considering a next move. Dash for the truck and bolt? "No, let's slow this down just a bit," I say. "We haven't eaten, and there's a Pancake House across the lot, past where the sedan is parked. Maybe we just wander over and get some food real quick."

"We can check out that car," Mike says.

"That's what I mean," I say, "let's do that. But let's go slow and not poke the bear. If it is a bear."

Rudy is silently mouthing, "Bear?"

Leaving bags behind we all exit the room, down the stairs, and start across the lot. Mike falls in at the far end of our line, with me and Rudy on the sedan side so he can side-eye it as we walk by, trying to look nonchalant.

Sure enough, there are two of them in there, two guys in suits watching us. We stroll on to the Pancake House, sit at the counter and quickly gobble stacks of pancakes. At one point Mike gets up and walks over to the kitchen doors, looking for a back way out. I'm thinking he might just bolt on foot, run like an Incan, head for the hills, but he doesn't. He returns and stands staring out at the sedan, weighing a walk back to the truck. All this time Rudy is watching him in rapt silence.

We pay our check, leave some jingle for the waitress, and walk back across the parking lot in reverse order, with Mike again on the far side watching the sedan with a fixed sidelong gaze. When we pass the car we see the two guys still inside staring back at us.

Back at the room – with no sign of the crazy-talk woman – we grab our stuff, take a breath, then out the door and into the truck, and out of the lot. Rudy in the middle, Mike in the jump seat ready to jump. The sedan pulls out and follows us out of the lot, onto the service road and up the ramp onto the interstate. It remains behind us for a few exits, Mike watching it intently in the truck's sideview mirror. Then after some minutes of silent panic he says "I think they're gone!"

We breathe a big sigh of relief and boom off toward Florida. Rudy asks "Who was that in that car?"

Mike says, "What car?"

We drop Rudy off in Jacksonville, where he's decided to visit a long-lost friend. He leaves wanting an explanation and knowing he wasn't going to get one. But I think hell, he's a writer, he can make one up.

Mike and I hurtle down the highway. I have an art auction to do in Miami. We check into a cheap roadside motel then head out to the venue, where he helps me unload and set up the artwork.

The auctioneer arrives – Harry Landers of TV fame *(Ben Casey, Combat,* and a long string of Taster's Choice commercials). Mike is chumming it up with some of the locals arriving for the big event. One of them is a cop, and they hit it off. Mike has a way with cops, though that doesn't always keep him out of jail.

Another newfound pal is a richly-dressed hipster doctor dude who gives Mike a lean joint of Maui-Wowee, which Mike slides into his shirt pocket for later.

The show goes on, a big success, with Harry moving over sixty-five thousand dollars worth of nicely-framed prints. As Mike and I are breaking down the show afterwards, Harry fills out paperwork and takes me aside to give me the standard big manila envelope with the receipts, a load of cash and checks. I realize that under no circumstances can I let Mike find out what's in the envelope, or leave it in any proximity to him, as its disappearance would put me right into a meat grinder. So I take it out to the truck and tuck it behind the driver's seat.

So now it's 2am or so, we're packed and rolling back toward the motel, and Mike pulls the joint out of his shirt pocket. We fire it up as we motor along and we're quickly getting faced, just stoned silly. I find the motel, pull into the parking lot, and we get out. We have the motel room key and the truck keys and I discretely grab the envelope, planning to stash it under my pillow.

But then the Hawaiian wave hits us hard and we're so stoned we're having functional issues, wandering around the truck trying to gather our things. Suddenly the motel key is gone missing – "Do you have it?" "I don't have it, you had it." "No I don't have it" – and now we're searching high and low for this key and I'm rummaging around the cab of the truck and I put the envelope on the hood of the truck so I can get down on my hands and knees and search underneath, no flashlight. Mike finally says "Fuck it, I'll get us in the bathroom window." An accomplished break-in artist, he quickly disassembles the window frame and climbs in, then comes around to unlock the door and let me in. And there we are, finally in the room, laughing hysterically, what a night, what a day, how about that weird woman, oh-

my-god this is the best grass I've ever had, and
we're soon conked out, snoring in our beds.

Mike awakes before me, late morning, stumbles
to the door in his underwear and looks out at
our truck. I'm still snoring. He says "Hey, you
left your envelope on the truck."

I'm awake instantly, one eye open wide.

He says "I'll put my pants on and go get it,
gotta piss first."

I say "Oh that's okay, I'll get it in a minute" and
while he's in the bathroom I'm up, pants on,
no shirt no shoes, skipping quickly over to the
truck to fetch the envelope full of cash. Right
there on the hood all night. Unbelievable luck.

I walk back as casual as I can muster, blinking
in the sudden bright of waking daylight as
Mike emerges from the bathroom. Showing
no big deal, no emotion, no nothing, I toss the
envelope onto my bed then take my turn in
the bathroom. In there I'm standing eyes closed,
listening, hoping he shows no further interest
in the envelope. And he doesn't – when I come

out of the bathroom he's got the TV on, sitting on his bed watching cartoons.

After breakfast Mike tells me he'll stay here in Miami – no way he's going back to New York right now. I tell him "Fine, brother – this is a good town for you." And I pack up quick before he changes his mind and make my way down the highway to the next show.

And as I drive away I'm thinking, this trip is supernatural. I've always had a lucky streak a mile wide. This one used every last inch.

I pass every hitchhiker the whole way home.

Lysergic Snowstorm

It was not my custom to bypass hitchhikers. Out of solidarity I pick up many while driving the art hauls for those months. Most are fairly short rides and most are not memorable, just simple hello and chatter and goodbye, good luck. But one goofy hitchhiker stands out.

It's early spring, which means mid-winter in the West Virginia mountains. I'm cruising eastward toward New York City on Interstate 68, skirting as much of Pennsylvania as possible, when I see a young red-haired kid with his thumb out. He reminds me of me.

I honk and slow, signal, check mirrors and move over a lane then onto the shoulder to stop. I watch him in the passenger side mirror as he runs for the truck, all gangly legs and arms akimbo, his knapsack thumping the back of his head over and over as he gallops.

Jimmy Longlegs jumps up into the cab with a huge toothy smile and thanks all over. He worms and wiggles, skinny and branchy, finally settling into a hunch over his knapsack. Back on the road, we share some laughs about hitching and I bask in his gratitude, his exuberant energy filling the cabin and warming my long driving day to a positive glow.

Jimmy is holding a book with both hands, clearly a precious thing. I ask him what he's reading and he holds up the cover – *Bartleby the Scrivener,* a small edition of the classic Melville story. He who prefers not to.

"I know it well!" I say, with a laugh – "love it actually – the slow dissolve of human spirit in early industrial times. Early Modern!"

"Well I've read it over and over," he says, "and I love it too but – the best is here inside."

"Which part?" I ask him.

Jimmy's smile widens evermore. He cracks *Bartleby* open to a certain page spread and holds the book flat, up to his face like a prayer book. Then he offers it toward me as a supplicant might. Taking quick glances while driving I see there's something in there, scattered along the inside seam of the book – what is that?

Jimmy dips his index finger into the seam
and comes out with a single tiny square of
windowpane, lysergic acid soaked into tiny
bits of paper. "It's really good," he assures me.

Unlike the scrivener – preferring to – I
gratefully consume. Thinking my long slog
will be more colorful now, I thank him and
bless his hipness. He isn't going far, so I soon
let him off with hand-slaps and big eye smiles
goodbye, a mutual moment of kinship in a
happy universe.

And off I go. It isn't many miles before snow
appears – a few big wet flakes at first, then
a virtual whiteout, traffic suddenly slowing.
An early spring blizzard blossoms around
us, coating the roads with thick slick snow
that slows traffic to a crawl. Visibility drops as
the snowfall thickens, with my lysergic also
blossoming such that I'm soon very keen on
the dimensionality of this whole endeavor –
shaped by the magic snow that is so heavy that
if I veer just outside of the tracks made by the
truck ahead of me, my truck begins to slide
sideways toward the edge of the roadbed.

Since panic serves no particular good purpose I decide to drive as an exercise in calm athletic fluidity instead. My truck is me. Relaxing into the motion and riding it, feeling the truck as an extension of my body and remaining very alert, I just drive. Slowly rolling, moment by moment, mile by mile, breathing deeply all the while, dazzled and humbled by the forces that have me in their grip. With a smile to match Jimmy's.

The animation of snow clouds flying and wind shaking the truck make for a delightful ride. Eventually I drive out of the squalls and across a bit of Pennsylvania and then New Jersey, heading for the Holland Tunnel. And that's when my personal blossom reaches its second peak – driving that truck through the bright grimy tunnel toward Manhattan with the clear sensation that I am, in fact, driving straight up. The tunnel is vertical, not horizontal. I'm convinced. But keep driving.

With upward mobility very much in mind, I wonder what it'll be like when I spill out onto Canal Street. Will that be downward? Sideways? No telling. If it's the moon we're heading to, guess we'll eat some green cheese when we get there.

And in the end, all slides smoothly. I miss the turn-off for the moon and instead navigate the truck through lower Manhattan, up to the Midtown Tunnel, and from there back to the Queens warehouse. All along the way the fabulous NYC lights dazzle. And now, with my sneakers back on solid (if breathing) ground, I stand awhile looking out over a dark parking lot – not completely dark, but with shimmering layers of faint light. It is a vibrating night ghost of a city I see, long gazing, feeling complete and one with it all.

Key West & Halfway Back

The year before I began driving trucks my brother Bill and I decide to hitchhike to Florida over our winter holiday break. It's a richly odd and eventful trip.

We catch a long ride down Interstate 95 and reach the Florida line in no time. At an RV campsite we ask if we can pitch our tent on their grass. The kid at the desk says "Sure" and gestures out to an empty patch a short way from the office. We pick a spot and drop our stuff, deciding to skip the tent and sleep out under the stars.

We're just falling asleep when a huge RV pulls up and begins backing towards us. With one eye barely open, then two wide open, I see his taillights heading our way. I roust my brother and jump out of my sleeping bag, shouting and waving my arms. The RV keeps coming. Billy jumps out of his sleeping bag and the two of us are waving and yelling, then we pound on the side of the RV and it stops. The driver jumps out in a huff – "What are you doing pounding on my RV?"

"You were gonna back over our heads!" we say.

"Yeah well, keep your hands off my coach!"

We fling a word or two at him then pick up our gear and move further away. And there we settle off to sleep.

In the morning our RV friend is repentant and offers us coffee and breakfast. His rig is something to behold, upholstered splendor. We're grateful for the food.

From there we continue south toward Miami, where we're drenched by a ferocious afternoon rainstorm and wander into a roadside diner to dry off and get something to eat. As we walk in, a charged quiet hangs in the air. No working staff in sight aside from one peeking out from the kitchen. A young family sits at a table, frozen in fear, as behind them a table full of bad-ass bikers are sprawled across chairs. One of the bikers is taking a bite from each of his french fries then bouncing the other half off the back of Dad's head. We stand there a moment, then turn and leave. Outside we look for a cop, with none in sight.

Further on, we cross miles of elevated highway on a series of hops – Largo, Islamorada, Marathon, Big Pine – until we reach Key West, where we camp with a bunch of hippies on a beach. The serene ocean air and lapping of waves is punctuated by the occasional roar of a Navy fighter jet taking off right above our heads. One early morning I enjoy my best cup of coffee ever, rich Cuban, watching the sunrise.

Sadly, as sometimes happens, we run out of money before running out of time. We save a single dime for an emergency call should things get really desperate. Heading north on empty bellies we do well with rides all the way through Miami and reach Fort Lauderdale. We head to the beach where people park their cars on the sand. There we walk and canvas the wheeled beachgoers – anyone heading north? Striking out and with afternoon rain due soon, we walk back to town and find the Salvation Army. Word has it they have free bunks and food.

By the time we arrive the rain is pounding. A small crowd of men stand outside the Salvation Army doors; inside the doors a retired Canadian Sergeant Major, stern fellow, stares at his watch, unwilling to let us in until the precise opening hour, 16:30. When he does let us in he lines us up and marches us into the dining room, where we're served bowls of pale soup and we're each handed one stale donut. At his signal we rise again, now to march into the chapel where a sermon and service await us. It features a remarkable family performance of evangelical music with a young boy on trumpet, his sister on flute, Dad on guitar and Mom on drums. Mom is a lively and disciplined drummer, with quick hands and a hair-do that never moves.

After service we march to the bunk room and it's lights out. Sergeant Major is a man of few words, but menacing eyes. Once he closes the door we break out three cans of beer from Billy's backpack and become very popular.

Crack of dawn Sergeant Major is back at the door. We march to breakfast – pale coffee, another stale donut – then out we go by 06:30. From there, back to the beach.

Our fortunes seem to change. We meet a group of young guys from upstate New York beside their big blue Buick. When we ask if they're heading north they huddle and confer, then tell us yes. I explain our situation and ask if they'll take us up to New York City. Another quick huddle and they agree we can ride along and help with the driving. There is, however, a strict protocol: we rotate drivers every hour on the hour and we keep the huge Family Bible in the center of the dashboard, where the driver has to peer around it to see. We quickly agree.

The bible boys are serious fellows. Each hour we stop to change drivers, which slows our forward progress. At one point I ask if maybe, on my next turn, can I drive for a few hours? They huddle then reply "No, we change drivers every hour. For safety!" So I agree to that and take my brief turns at the wheel.

Billy does likewise but he's annoyed with these guys and their rigidity, as well as their bible chatter. His next turn he gets behind the wheel and peels off. Once up to speed he grabs the Family Bible and tosses it onto the seat between us. "I can't see around that," he tells them. But they're already in a serious whisper huddle over this offense. Breaking from the huddle they inform us that they've decided to change their route and will be dropping us off in Pennsylvania in a few hours.

I tell them that's fine, but please, whoever's driving, please stop near an off-ramp so we can walk to an on-ramp and continue hitching.

Once we reach Pennsylvania, with one of them behind the wheel and increasing hostility in the car, the driver suddenly swerves off to the shoulder and orders us out.

"This is a terrible spot," I tell him.

"Out," they say.

So we gather our stuff and exit the car, Billy tossing a few choice words at them on his way.

So now we're up on the interstate where we cannot hitch. The first cop who sees us doing that will nail us. So we're walking back toward the last exit we passed a few miles back, and we're almost there when a Pennsylvania trooper pulls over and flips on his lights. He tells us he's going to write us for hitchhiking. "But we're not," I say, "we're just walking back to the exit to get on the on-ramp.

We know better than to hitch up here on the highway." He shakes his head, writes us two tickets, then tells us to get in the cruiser and he'll drive us to the on-ramp.

The rest of the trip home is relatively easy. I decide I'm not paying the Pennsylvania hitchhiking ticket and never do.

The Blockade

So it is, a year later, that I find myself behind
the wheel of a commercial truck, driving
Interstate-80 eastward through Akron, Ohio
and facing the prospect of the long homeward
slog through Pennsylvania to reach Long Island.
They need my leftover art back at the warehouse
to load other shows and they need me there as
soon as possible. So my usual habit of avoiding
Pennsylvania entirely is entirely out of the
question. I'll have to traverse it – eight hours end
to end, not daring to drive over 55 for fear of
an arrest warrant from that unpaid hitchhiking
ticket. All it'll take is a traffic stop by a state
trooper and I'll find myself out of a job, maybe a
short jail stay, who knows.

I'd taken the Collier trucking job the previous
summer by answering a newspaper ad for
long-haulers. An art company hired me to
drive straight rigs full of framed artwork to
hometown auctions all across the eastern half of
the nation, eventually to the west coast as well.
The firm was owned by two brothers, Mike
and Irving – Mike opened a gallery in west
L.A., and Irv opened a New York warehouse

to handle the eastern half of the country. It was a gallery in the broadest sense – two large warehouses full of paintings, prints and small sculptures and truck bays. The west coast office has an atelier where artists execute editions in lithograph and other media. The business involves booking art auctions as fund raisers for social organizations and sending out loads of art to link up with auctioneers hither and yon. Office-bound bookers cold-call Rotaries, Moose lodges, hospitals, United Way branches and the like, offering the opportunity for a gala social event featuring classy artwork to be sold at auction, following a heavy-handed cocktail hour, with the host organization taking a small cut of the proceeds. The art is mostly decorative pieces by unknown artists or art factories, with a sprinkling of high-ticket items – limited edition prints and oils by better-known artists.

Collier provides a truckload of this catalogued art and an auctioneer, many of whom are TV actors padding uneven Hollywood income by taking on these weekend road auctions. Grueling work for them – they have to coax crowds they never wanted to see, crowds they hoped would be watching them on the big screen but instead eyeball them at the local civic center. For us drivers it's a truck loaded with two or three shows — about 200 pieces per show — and a long haul to arrive on time for the load-in, the set-up, and then, in shirt and tie, working the auction on stage with the auctioneer. We place each item on an easel, bathed in light, for the auctioneer to make casual remarks and work the crowd for bids.

My favorite auctioneer is Harry Landers, who drinks straight vodka from a Collins glass (splash of water, splash of tonic) and teases the crowd with airs of high living, seducing wives into goading husbands to bid on living room masterpieces. Harry had a small role in the Alfred Hitchcock film *Rear Window* in 1954, and his celebrity grew as Dr. Ted Hoffman, sidekick to Vince Edwards' TV doctor on the *Ben Casey* series, a medical drama that ran from 1961 to 1966. But Harry's star burned most brightly as spokesman for Taster's Choice coffee in television commercials that aired into the 1970s. He and I worked together mid-1970's, when the acting and shilling gigs were fewer, further between, and located not in Hollywood, but in places like Opelousas, Louisiana.

I pick up my manifest envelope at the warehouse one morning and find my way to Opelousas for a Friday night auction at the Yamatorium, which turns out to be a massive old airplane hangar become ersatz civic center. Opelousas is in St. Landry Parish and claims to be the Yam Capitol of the World, hence the naming of the hangar. It is celebrated today as the spiritual center of Zydeco music, the home of Clifton Chenier, the king of Zydeco.

When I arrive at the Yamatorium on that March mid-afternoon the Louisiana air is sopping wet and oppressive – I can only imagine what it must be like here in August. I start unloading the truck myself, carrying artwork into the hall and arranging it on long folding tables set up in a crescent around the vast open space of the hall. The host women then provide me with a couple of helpers, as was our custom, and we're all sweating hard after just a few minutes of unloading. The Yamatorium has an incredibly tall ceiling – well over a hundred feet high at center – below which hang these huge industrial air conditioning units. We ask if the AC could be put on and it is, the huge suspended units booming into action. Soon the temperature in there is dropping like a stone and we complete the set-up with renewed vigor.

By the time the crowds begin filtering in for the cocktail hour – men in light suits, women in bright dresses – the Yamatorium is thoroughly chilled and the guests request that the AC be turned off, which it is.

As the cocktail hour ends and the crowd takes roost in folding chairs, Harry busies himself while I cart the first load of paintings up onto the stage. He begins with his usual pre-show banter, the cemented smile and soft grumble dropping Hollywood names and laying out ground rules between sips of vodka.

I place the first painting on the easel and stand back, gazing out over the vast space and the eager crowd while Harry's magic goes into second gear – swirling tales of the *Ecole de Paris* and the "once-in-a-lifetime opportunity to own such a fine work as this, just picture it over your sofa, in your den, handed down to your children, its value ever increasing, oops I didn't mean to open the bidding that low, my mistake, but yes, since I said it, I will have to honor a ridiculously low opening bid of $250 on this priceless work – quick, take it off the easel, Kelly, before someone – well darn, we have a bid…"

As he rattles on I sense the air becoming heavy and fuzzy. It's slowly fogging as the temperature rises in the Yamatorium. As I stand there gazing out at the vast space, a small but defined cloud is forming up there in the rafters, around the silent AC units. The cloud thickens, gets darker and more distinct. I gaze in wonder.

Then it begins to rain inside the Yamatorium, our little cloud sending tiny needle-like raindrops that quickly form thin puddles on the concrete floor.

Mouth agape, Harry squints out at a cloud-banked crowd, slipping now from the palm of his hand as they hustle to cover up against the tropical indoor weather. They flee en masse out into the drier outdoor air. The Yamatorium drains of people and Harry sags. I scramble to cover the soaking artwork curling up in its frames, my dress shoes sliding like ice skates on the slick floor.

So that is my day-to-day life, driving up and down the east coast, and out to the midwest, with my loads of alleged art and Harry's monologues. I carefully avoid Pennsylvania, taking longer routes whenever necessary to get around it.

But this one time I can't avoid it. From near Chicago, I call in to the office before setting off homeward. They tell me it's urgent that I get back to New York as fast as I can – "we'll pay your speeding tickets," they always said – because they need the leftover art on my truck for other shows that need to go out fast. I agree to leave right away and realize there is really no way I can avoid the Commonwealth of Pennsylvania.

I-80 runs east-west across the Commonwealth from the Ohio state line near Sharon PA to the Delaware Water Gap Toll Bridge over the Delaware River and into New Jersey, straight to New York. I-80 through north-central Pennsylvania can seem like the longest road ever laid on earth. An interminable ride with little to see and with long stretches of worst possible places to break down. But I've gotten past all that on a long slow day, kicked back but alert

for troopers, watching my speed carefully. By
nightfall I'm within seven miles of the Jersey
line, feeling big and nearly home-free.

But then a girl runs out of the woods into
the edge of my headlights. Waving her arms,
panicked. I just barely see her as I'm gliding by,
then quickly jerk the truck over and stop on
the shoulder. The passenger door is unlocked so
before I actually see her again, she flings it open
and jumps up into the cab. Hysterical. Crying,
shouting and laughing more or less all at once.
Instant pandemonium.

She's screaming, "Thank you! I love you!! New
York City!!!"

I check my side mirror then start off onto the
highway. She gradually settles a bit, and when
I turn on the cab light I see she's wet herself. I
figure her age as maybe twenty – she's a big girl,
and bedraggled, but calming enough now that
we can begin to converse. I ask her where she's
come from, and what was happening, but don't
get any coherent explanation for her run from
the woods.

I ask her where she's going. She says, "New York!"

"Where in New York?"

"Umm, the candy store," she says. "Two doors down – apartment 37!"

"Manhattan? Brooklyn? The Bronx?"

"The candy store," she says.

Oh. So I'm thinking, how many candy stores in all the five boroughs? And realizing that my passenger, by turns quiet then loud and effusive, is not of sound mind. She has no idea where she's going. And I can't just drop her somewhere in New York, she'll get eaten alive. What am I going to do?

My answer appears up ahead, as we approach the toll booths at the Jersey state line.

I see police lights spinning, lots of them – a blockade across all the lanes. Troopers are gathered on both sides, with one standing in our lane, pointing at me with his other hand up. Stop!

Oh man. Here I am, an eighth of a mile from freedom, and I'm not gonna make it. I have this young lady sputtering gibberish beside me, still telling me she loves me. I stop and the cop approaches my window.

He sees the fear and confusion on my face and the first thing he says to me is, "Don't worry, you're not in trouble."

"I'm not?"

"One of our troopers saw you stop and pick her up," he says.

"She came running out of the woods like she was in trouble," I say. "I stopped to help her and she jumped in the truck."

I look over at her. Now she seems coiled and ready to strike.

"She wants me to take her to New York," I say to the trooper, "but she doesn't know where in New York. I can't just drop her off somewhere..."

He stops me. "Those woods," he says, "behind

those woods is a state hospital. She walked away. We'd like to remove her from your truck and take her back to the hospital."

"Oh please do," I say, "because I don't know where to bring her."

With that she uncoils. The love-talk turns to rampage, she's punching me in the shoulder now, cursing and kicking, crazy eyes. I'm doing my best to duck her punches but she lands a few. Girl can punch!

Two other troopers yank her door open and reach in to pull her out. They tangle, she's big but quick. She gets a couple of good punches off them too before they get her out and onto the ground. One of the cops reaches up and slams the door shut.

The blessed cop at my window is saying, "Go! Go! Just go on through the booth, don't stop for the toll, just go!"

I hit the gas and lurch toward salvation, my wheels barely touching the ground.

A Hop and a Skip to Iowa

Skip and I go way back, almost all the way. We attended kindergarten together, then elementary and high school. He went off to Iowa for undergrad study in molecular biology, while I went for North American literature at SUNY Oneonta, Buffalo, and McGill University in Montreal. We kept in close touch and he made his way to McGill for grad work. We shared in wintry joys among the lively and proud Quebecois.

But prior to that, we're both on summer break – early summer 1974 – and decide to hitch out to Iowa to see his school buds in Des Moines. The trip out is not memorable, just short and long hops with strangers kind and strange. Once we get there, our Iowa stay is sun-blessed, me amazed at all the flatness, it just goes on and on. Skip's friends are lively and kind, in for a laugh. I have a photo Skip made on that trip with a tulip blossom looming over me, about to knock me over, taken from the ground up with Skip on his back in the garden. A keeper.

The hitching highlight of that trip is the glorious homeward return. After a string of short hops gets us into Illinois, a classic Chevy panel truck – the kind an old-fashioned plumber might use – pulls over and honks us in. Barry from Denver and his enormous German Shepherd, Sarge, are heading all the way to Jersey and happy to have our company. Sarge is a sweet beast, calm and friendly, not bothered by the travel, just keen to be by Barry's side. The truck is late-1950s vintage with a throttle knob on the dashboard, so Barry throttles it up and sits sideways with his legs on the passenger seat, the better to share conversation with us in the back whilst keeping an occasional eye on the long straight road ahead. The rear of the truck is laden with soft rugs and blankets, a flying cloud upon which to curl away for a nap or lay out straight to eye-surf head-first down the highway.

Barry happens to have a bag of hooch tucked under his dashboard. Soon joints are rolled and we roll blissfully eastward toward morning. The panel truck only does about 55 or 60mph so it's a long slow go. We cycle driving shifts with naps in back but mostly fill time with story, joke, opinion, philosophy, speculation, wonderment, and low-ball collective wisdom. We decide we've pretty much worked it all out by the time we reach the Jersey line.

Skip has a trove of photographs he made along the way, with us taking roadside breaks and drinking from big jugs of Denver water. We have a glorious slow road together, finding peace and a happy grace among good company.

A year later, I fly into Denver to attend a writers jamboree up in Boulder. Barry picks me up at the airport, kindly takes me home for a simple dinner and a restful night on their couch. As deep western hippies of the time he and his bride Sara live complex lives simply, with gratitude and beatitude, valuing all they have, always ready to share.

Toward Heaven Above

Decades later, I'm in Catalunya with local friends. On a breezy Saturday afternoon in Cubelles, Anna and I are walking a dusty side road to a larger road to hitchhike from her family's farm to the village, to catch a train back to Barcelona.

The farm has been in Anna's family for generations, serving as a refuge during the worst of the Spanish civil war when Franco was bombing Barcelona. Now it's home to uncles and a gathering spot for all of the family on holidays. Wide, open and arid, with large farming plots, fruit trees, and olive trees, the farm is bordered on all sides by a stout stone wall. During the war the mayor used to bring a chicken every Sunday, which fed everyone. The farm and Cubelles sustained them.

I met Anna a year earlier while hitchhiking through Ireland. We chatted at a bus stop and then took a train together back to Dublin, packed in with kids heading to a U2 show. Anna's not keen on hitchhiking and thinks me a bit crazy for doing it, but on this relaxed Catalan

Saturday she relents because there's no one available to take us. She knows Cubelles and the local people and she's comfortable here.

And as local fate has it, standing roadside with our thumbs in the air, her brother Carles drives by and swerves to pick us up. He's heading for another town closer to Barcelona, Vilanova i la Geltrú, just one stop before Sitges. After a lively drive he drops us off at the north end of Vilanova and we begin a short hike through the center of town to the train station.

As we walk along we encounter small groups of people, then throngs, a deep festive crowd gathering as we make our way toward the center of town. When we reach the plaza it's jammed with festive locals and teams of Castellers, the builders of human castles – towers of men standing atop each others' shoulders, often five, six, or seven stories tall.

We linger, amazed by our good fortune in finding this on our way to catch a train. They're just setting up, getting ready to build castles. We see three distinct teams of Castellers, each with brightly-hued tunics and sashes. As we meander among them they're swaddling each other in the long sashes, turning them tightly around each others' mid-sections. They wind the fabric carefully so that each man has firm bracing for his back and gut. The sash also serves as toe hold and finger hold for climbers.

Once all are wrapped they gather to assemble the tower, forming a wide ring of the biggest men as the base. They jostle into a tight circle, close beside each other, flexing their arms across each other's shoulders, tucking in and bracing their legs to form a solid foundation.

As the base ring settles, the other two teams of Castellers – sixty to eighty men in all – move in close behind them. They're lending their collective mass for support, while forming a safety net of hands and arms that can reach up to catch the falling.

A second ring of men then climb up using their toes in the sashes and their hands to grasp. Stepping up onto the shoulders of the base men they form a wobbly tenuous ring and slowly settle as each man finds his balance, and as the base adjusts to take their weight. Soon the second ring is stable, all arms locked tightly across the shoulders of adjacent neighbors. The wobble settles.

Next ring up – fewer men, a higher climb, sash to shoulder, more wobble as they all stand tall, then settle.

Two more rings go up. At five levels, they stand as tall as some of the buildings facing the plaza.

Two smaller men scuttle up sashes and shoulders and take their place at the top as the final ring, settling into a mutual balance. The bottom holds steady. All up and down the tall pyramid, men stand firm with nary a wiggle.

At their highest competitive levels, the world record is nine levels of men in a standing pyramid. Our Castellers are local, they compete on special occasions. Here, as we encounter them in the village plaza, they're not really competing – it's more like a friendly three-way scrimmage.

Looking around us at all the eager faces, we come to realize an even-more-special occasion is happening. A young girl, six or seven years

old, is stepping out from the press of her family
wearing a little helmet. She is about to make
her first ascent to the top. We stand there at the
jam-packed base in awe of what we're seeing.

As they built the tower, the Castellers moved
and worked slowly, wobbling toward balance.
This little athlete has none of that. She launches
herself up the backs of those men, moving
quickly and surely, small brave fingers and toes
grasping sashes and shoulders, pulling herself up
the tower really fast, graceful and fearless.

When she reaches the top, she climbs up onto
the final shoulder and with a flourish swings
one leg across the top, turns upright and throws
her arm into the air with a victory fist. Then
she scrambles down as artfully as she'd ascended.

As she touches the ground, beaming, a roar of
applause erupts from hundreds of assembled
family, neighbors and friends with hugs and
her family's tears all around. A rite of passage
completed, witnessed by all who know and care
for her.

So remarkable it is to walk up on a scene like that and witness all the pride in the occasion. As we ride the train back to Barcelona we talk about it, still astonished at what we'd seen. That young girl hitching her way up to heaven, to the very top of the castle, crossing generations' backs and shoulders skyward, and her brave fist at the very top. Momentous!

A few days later we're hiking up a mountain in the Pyrenees. We'd planned an early departure that morning to start the long hike early, but then took our time getting going and dallied a bit along the way, walking through shops. By the time we get to the mountain it's past noon, the day sun-blasted but chilly at that altitude. We dilly-dally some more at the base station, then begin hiking. Moving laterally upward on a meandering track, we come upon a dusty road snaking up the mountainside. Some sips of water then up the road we go, enlivened by fresh alpine air, stopping to soak in breathtaking vistas all around.

But I'm also watching the weather. We're dressed lightly, wearing just a few springtime layers. It gets late early here, with air temps dropping like stone. Stepping down a mountain in the dark is not a good idea.

So I say to Anna, "We're not gonna make it to the top. It'll be close to dark by the time we get there, and I don't want us coming down in darkness." She agrees. "Let's go just a bit more," she says, "then we can turn around."

We continue on and up and before long I think I hear a rumble, faint at first but slowly growing. I turn and gaze down the mountain to see a stunning sight – a gigantic, many-wheeled, all-terrain cement truck is growling its way up the road toward us. Must be pouring concrete up at the ski lifts. I'm gripped now by the realization of this top-ten-ever hitchhiking opportunity – the chance to hitch a cement truck to the top of a mountain.

So I call to Anna and tell her, "Look! Our ride to the top! Just smile and put out your thumb," I say, "maybe wiggle your leg out a little..."

She laughs, at first astonished, then appalled.

"No!" she says. "No! Jeddy! I am a feminist!"

The mixer monster of the mountaintop is roaring closer now. And what do they say in basketball? You miss every shot you don't take. So I step forward and throw down the thumb, looking up at the driver with what I hope is a winning smile.

His return glare tells me he'd just as soon run me over as pick us up. Off he goes, roaring past, blessing us in dust.

Oh Well

It's one of those inside-your-head phrases
familiar to hitchhikers. Oh well – no one's going
to pick me up here, I better start walking. As an
alternative to frustration and despair, it works.
Oh well – just keep going. Onward!

This most fabulous hitching opportunity, though
a failure, remains a vivid memory. Hiking a
mountain, our climbing mojo fading toward
"oh well" when a giant cement truck rises like a
dragon savior, but sadly, passes us by.

It might have been the best ride ever. Instead it's
the young VW bus hippie who worked for The
Band up in Saugerties, our glide across the pink
sky bridge, homeward.

Road Surfing Portugal

I'm mulling over the metaphor of hitchhiking as road surfing – riding waves of human generosity and trust that fluctuate with the wind, the weather, and the news. It can leave you bobbing in slack water with time to contemplate sharks.

My youngest niece Corinne, having completed her undergraduate studies in the spring of 2016, decides she's ready for a grand adventure – a solo tour of Europe in the classic hostel-to-hostel backpacking style. With her parents supportive but disconcerted by the lack of a detailed plan – she's going to stop in Iceland for a few days, then... "wherever" – we conspire to add some structure to Corinne's trip by arranging to meet up with her – her mom and dad in Dublin, her sister Kate in Greece, and me in Portugal. I'm ready for some time off and a bit of adventure giving my hitching thumb another workout in a foreign country. Corinne and I set a date to rendezvous in Lisbon.

I'd been to Catalunya numerous times but never to the Atlantic side of the Iberian Peninsula.

Along with the delight of traveling with a young adventurer making her first solo foray out in a larger world, I see an opportunity to further my hitchhiking career in a new country. A new chapter to my adventures as a beggar of rides, jumping into the cars of strangers to see if human kindness still exists in this particular way and place. The Atlantic coast of Portugal is Europe's hottest surfing spot, with a commercialized surf culture exploding in recent years, so it seems the right locale to ride the road surfing analogy.

I arrive in Lisbon on an Air Canada flight from Columbus through Toronto. And there she is – her face beaming among the throng of sign-wavers outside customs. She'd arrived a day earlier and had already explored local transit, so she guides me through crowds of luggage-loaded arrivistes to the Aeroporto de Lisboa Metro station. From there we venture into the oldest city core in Western Europe (Lisbon's origins predate those of London, Paris and Rome by several centuries, we learn). I'd arranged for an AirBNB near the Museu Calouste Gulbenkian, just north of the Old City, le Bairro Alto.

Arriving at the Baixa-Chiado station, we make our way to the street and wander, happily disoriented, with the aid of a compass and a good old-fashioned paper map. Along the way we discover that the Portuguese will gladly give directions even when they do not know exactly where you want to go. That lengthens our search a bit, with some false turns and doubling back. But we do eventually find Avenida João Crisóstomo, and there encounter another challenge not unknown to early AirBNBers: we find our destination (a six-story apartment building) but the apartment number and contact information for our host are locked up in my iPhone, which has died en route. Luckily someone exits the building and lets us in, and in the lobby we decide to take the brute force approach – we'll knock on every door until we find the right one. Working our way up from floor to floor, we startle a number of older Portuguese women before arriving at the top, where our smiling host Alinea is waiting for us.

The flat is lovely – homey, comfortable, and clean, with a well-stocked kitchen. We're sharing it with one other person, a freelance journalist named Simon who lives nearby in

Lisbon but is AirBNBing while his own flat is being renovated. Simon is a New European – German-born, holds a Swiss passport, has worked for years in Africa while living in Portugal. We share some time with him that afternoon and again in the morning at his favorite cafè down on the street.

Simon is a young "old Portugal hand," having lived among its post-colonial African legacy, and has many questions about the political season back in the States. He is, I should note, skeptical about my plans to hitchhike up the Portugal coast – "No one will pick you up," he advises. "It just isn't done here anymore." Nor back in the U.S., I tell him, and yet I wonder whether I might be able to make a go of it – it seems a relic now of a not-long-gone past, when I'd hitched all across the U.S. and parts of Europe, and I wonder why.

"People are too scared now," he says, and I have to agree that it seems so. And that is truly the topic I'm exploring – what has changed so radically in the last thirty years that a common cultural function like hitchhiking is now looked upon as crazy, when in my youth it was accepted both in the U.S. and abroad. With hitchhiking the arc is outwards toward discovery. The thrust is human trust being tested.

In any event, I'm not going to hitchhike with my niece along, nor encourage her to do so. She and I venture out to explore Lisbon on foot and via the Metro and tram. We find a throng of tourists in the Barrio Alto and jump a tram to escape to the less-explored margins of the city, just east of the Golden Gate-style 25 de Abril bridge. There we find our best meal of our Lisbon stay at Restaurante-Cervejaria O Palacio *(Marisco sempre fresquissimo* – Fish always fresh). A humble, local sort of place, not a tourist in sight, specializing of course in fish. Corinne digs into a marvelous grilled salmon with boiled potatoes while I go for grilled octopus. It is fresh, perfectly done, not chewy as overcooked *polvo* can be, but moist and delicious, tasting of the sea.

After a second day exploring Lisbon on foot, Corinne and I hop a train to Cascais, where we stay at another AirBNB and explore this seaside suburb linking Lisbon to the beautiful beaches along the Atlantic coast.

I'm delighted to see Corinne cracking the egg of international travel, to watch her figure out solutions to language and navigation problems. Her easy, outgoing personality serve her well, she makes fast friends among other backpackers. While hitchhiking may have lapsed into history, backpacking certainly has not. Hostels all across Europe are full of young global citizens exploring new worlds, hauling life's scant necessities on their backs.

After several days of carefree exploration and adventurous eating, it's bittersweet to see Corinne leave for the Lisbon airport in a midnight cab. She has, in her last-minute planning, booked a number of crack-of-dawn flights without thinking of the need to get from Point-A, B or C to the airport at 6am. She's processed that lesson while sleeping in various airports, forgoing the lap of luxury for lessons learned the more memorable way, and is now happily decamped to Croatia.

Once she departs it's my mission to test the journalist's prediction that no one in Portugal will pick up an aging American hitchhiker.

But first I'll do a nice long hike along the seaside highway. I walk out the coast road from Cascais toward Guincho, passing Cabo de Roca, the westernmost point of continental Europe. I carry some water and a notebook. The day is chilly with a fierce wind driving off the water, heavy waves exploding up along the rock shoreline, and salt spray touching my face on the far side of the road, eighty yards from shore.

I'm standing roadside, across from a deep stretch of rock beach with waves crashing. I spot a sign nearer the water's edge, a pictogram signaling danger? I can't quite make it out from this distance, so I cross the road and walk down the rock ledge for a closer look. Now I see the pictogram is a figurative human looking straight up at a giant wave claw about to snatch him away. Gazing out at the roiling water, I shiver at the thought – a quick end you'd hope, as you'd be dashed against the rocks before being sucked out to sea for your eternal rest. I cross the road, gather up my pack and make for higher ground.

With the hike now nearing ten kilometers, I take a break at a small seaside restaurant and eat a bowl of vegetable soup and some bread.

A young family comes in as I'm eating and sits near me, and when I hear them talking I call over – "Americans! You're the first I've seen in a week. Where are you from?"

Friendly, they respond and we chat for a few minutes. Turns out he completed his undergrad studies at a small Ohio college not 30 miles from my current home. Small world, as we say.

Leaving the restaurant and heading back toward Cascais, I decide to put the Lisbon journalist's words to the test. I turn to walk backwards and throw out my thumb in the universal hitchhiking signal. And here I must report, FLASH, the very first car that appears around the bend screeches to a halt and throws open a door. Gonçalo, a sculptor and art professor at the University of Aveiro, is riding with his bride Adelina back to Cascais from Guincho. They happily take me aboard and pepper me with questions about the U.S.

It's a good sign, I decide. Maybe my plan to hitchhike north along the coast isn't so hopeless.

The next morning I arise early, load my backpack and head out. I packed light before leaving the States, knowing I'd be hitchhiking and therefore walking many miles. For my five-week excursion I have one pair of quick-dry slacks, a couple pair of shorts, two t-shirts and one wrinkle-resistant dress shirt, two pair of socks, and two of underwear. The largest and heaviest article is my wetsuit, as I planned to do some surfing and knew the early-summer Atlantic would be cold. I also carry a small kit with a toothbrush and razor, my notebook, and one cherished book to read along the way – Peter Matthiessen's *Shadow Country*. It is, in all, a twenty pound load – not bad. I know I'll have to curb my penchant for collecting rocks, my favored travel souvenirs.

I leave Cascais along N247, walking west toward Cabo de Roca and Guincho – the reverse of the route Gonçalo had taken me the day before. I cover several kilometers, enjoying the fresh air while hitching, listening during long moments of no traffic for the roar behind the silence. It is a soundtrack I've heard before – the song of the seas woven into a light fabric of hope and expectation, Earth and the universe calling. My goal is to reach Ericeira, a locus for the burgeoning surf culture that has grown along

the area's rock beaches. I'm alert for cars with
surfboards on the roof, thinking I'll connect
with some surfers heading my way. Instead,
after watching BMW and Mercedes drivers
avoid my gaze, a small Honda pulls over and
a woman scrambles to clear her passenger seat
of maps and other debris. She is Cinzia, in her
forties perhaps, a happy Italian vacationing
from her job in Milano. Her English is not so
good, she apologizes, and we cheerfully make
conversation in a mix of Italian, Spanish and
English, using gestures to fill in missing bits.
She's met some young guys in Cascais and is
heading off to a rendezvous in Sintra, which
means she can take me about ten kilometers
before turning off. I tell her that's great. Then
after several minutes of easy conversation
she offers to take me all the way to Ericeira
– after all, she's not in a rush and is open to
unexpected detours along her way. So I offer to
buy us lunch in exchange and she agrees that
will be great.

A little while later we stop near Colares at a
beachside restaurant and have some olives, bread,
cheese and wine, filling brief silences with
thoughtful gazes out at the beautiful sea. Back in

the car we circle around, get lost and find ourselves back at the restaurant – we share a good laugh about that. We use her map and my compass to get ourselves back on track and slowly wind our way northwards through slender inland valleys back to the coast, toward Ericeira.

I'm expecting a small beach town. But we roll into something else – an ancient village core overwhelmed by new development, with tile-roofed apartments and condos in all directions, far as the eye can see. I'd heard of the great surfing spots along the Portugal coast, but did not realize its scope until Ericeira. Here, surfing has exploded into a mass culture phenomenon, and places like this and nearby Rebeira – declared a World Surfing Reserve in 2011 – are now Wetsuit Disneyland chocked with surf camps, surf villas, surf shops and surfing schools. Yikes, I think. My vision of a serene beach and rolling waves dotted with a few surfers is more like rush hour at Surf City. That whole road surfing idea suddenly loses its hold on me.

Cinzia drives us into the heart of town and insists on buying us a beer as thanks for lunch. We sit in the sun and take in the spectacle, with me feeling quite let down by what I'm seeing but grateful nonetheless for her generosity and kindness in getting me here. We bid adieu and she motors off to Sintra while I hoist my backpack and go looking for a surf flophouse with a spare room.

I find it up a side road across from Rebeira d' Ilhas. Tiago, the host, is one of the early surfing denizens of the area, having moved here from Lisbon in search of the perfect wave in the early 1970s. A small band of dedicated surfers coalesced around this beach after some long-haired Australians showed up in a VW "bread loaf" microbus with surfboards strapped to the roof. Local fishermen were bemused but also fascinated. What are these crazy fellows doing, riding the waves on these boards? The fishermen think perhaps surfboards might provide a convenient new way for them to take a mid-day lunch break without having to haul in their boats – just skim on in to shore, have some lunch, and skim back out. But after watching the surfers they realize it's not so simple as that. And as local kids like Tiago begin to emulate the Aussies, hijacking ironing boards and fences, local authorities spring into action. The magistrate begins issuing summonses for reckless behavior and disturbing the peace, with police confiscating the homemade surfboards. But to their credit, the parents of the neophyte surfer kids rally, marching into city hall to demand the police end their harassment. What is the harm? They are simply being kids in a new way!

After some debate between village council and the magistrate, the mayor declares that surfing will be allowed on one section of the beach and the official sanctions will end.

As Tiago tells it, soon after hearing reports from visiting surfers of the world-class breaks at Rebeira, the founders of the Australian surf wear company Billabong decided to set up a shop in Ericeira. It seemed a questionable move at the time – Rebeira was remote and unknown to all but the most dedicated surfers around the world. But no longer. The shop helps spur a local and global breakout of commercial surfing and all goods related. It's now a landmark among an old guard of surfers, who mourn the loss of their beloved breaks to the urban mobs.
Tiago is a pushed-aside legacy of burgeoning commercial culture – his original surfing school

is now but one among two hundred in the area. Small, wiry and wily, a keen observer of the surf, Tiago waits for good conditions to guide his students out into the breaks and carve some curls. The newcomer schools operate in all conditions – they'll take you out whenever you show up to bob around on flat water.

A German film crew has most of the rooms at Tiago's flop, but I crash there for a day and do a little surfing even though conditions aren't great. I grew up body surfing on sandy bottoms – here you're surfing above rock. As Tiago tells me, "Bail early."

My disconcerted first reaction to Ericeira is confirmed by Tiago's reports of the fading glory of this once-special, now too-special place. I relate the famous Yogi Berra remark about a St. Louis restaurant – "No one goes there anymore, it's too crowded" – and he returns a rueful laugh. Past the point of searching for a new secret spot and starting over, he's committed to hanging in and doing his best to do things the right way, right here, like a partner who cannot bring himself to leave the lover who's gone mad and thrown all the bedding out into the street.

I leave Ericeira in a doleful rain. The road north to Peniche runs along the coast, carrying little traffic on this soggy morning, so I'm standing in a drizzle, hovering weightless and wet, waiting for nothing to happen. So I walk, hoping for a luckier spot. A small car lurches to a stop beside me, crammed full of Portuguese working men, all drunk. There's really no place to put me but they're smiling, soused, waving me in. I decide no, as desperate as I am for a ride, not this ride. I shake my head no, smile back at them and wave them on. They laugh and drive off.

I walk some more. The drizzle stops, then restarts. Fog gathers, dissipates and recovers. I'm lost in thought when another car pulls over, driven by a young woman. She waves me in.

It's such a relief to get into that car. The driver is bright and lively, chipper, and speaks English well. She's a yoga instructor driving to a class a few miles ahead. I tell her I'm heading to Peniche and she says she's going up there after her class. "If I see you roadside later," she says, "I'll pick you up again."

My next encounter is a keeper. A truck pulls up, the driver flings open the door. Rigo the fisherman is hauling his catch to Docapesca, the commercial fish market at Peniche. Rodrigo Martes runs three fishing boats – his largest, he tells me, is the Tee-tin-ick.

"Tee-tin-ick?" I say, thinking it's Portuguese.

He says, "You know, like the movie?"

I say, "Oh, Titanic? So you're not superstitious?" He just laughs, tells me I can come work on his fishing boat. I'm tempted in the moment.

I ride along with him to the busy fish docks and help him unload bins of skate. He carts them into the market and I sit awhile in the brightly colored bleachers for the fish auction, watching a host of commercial buyers bidding on the numbered bins after careful inspections.

Later, leaving the fish market, I'm thankful for the *leite da bondade humana* I find among the Portuguese. I stroll with my pack past the marina and across a small bridge, where Peniche points like a thumb out into the Atlantic just a few miles south of Nazaré, the famed surfing spot where top big wave surfers from Hawaii have ridden the Earth's largest waves, sometimes out to the eternal sea.

After several easy days of hitchhiking between local surfing hotspots I take a train up to the fabulous old city of Porto. There at the Estação São Bento train station I gaze at spectacular blue-tile azulejo murals of Portugal's early rural character and the Battle of *Arcos de Valdevez*.

Up on the train platform, I notice phrases tiled into the floors reading *Por favor, não alimente os pombos* ("Please do not feed the pigeons").

Looking up at a distant cliff wall facing the station, I see giant hand-painted graffiti urging the contrary, in English: FEED THE PIGEONS.

For me, that expresses the true nature of the gentle Portuguese: generous; a bit rebellious; endowed with a great, dark-eyed humor; and welcoming to winged and hitchhiking strangers.

Closer to God and What Comes Next

Hitchhiking requires a vehicle, but not necessarily a car. Boats, airplanes, horses – anything that moves forward, backward or sideways – can be hitched. It's been done on all of those conveyances, as well as on divers form of motorcycle, truck, and tractor. It was a joke and a very short ride, but I once caught a thumb-out on a shopping cart.

In Ireland, a boat provided my most excellent ride. I hitchhiked down to Cahirciveen, a tiny fishing town in southwestern Ireland in County Kerry, astride the River Ferta. What drew me to Cahirciveen was Mike Boaz' advice to hitchhike those extra miles into the far Gaelic reaches to see the Skelligs – two towering rock crags rising out of the sea eight miles offshore.

Once you reach Cahirciveen you get out to the Skelligs by hitching a ride on a fishing boat. If the seas aren't too rough, a fisherman will drop you off on Skellig Michael and retrieve you at the end of his workday for a few Irish punts.

The Skellig Rocks – Skellig Michael and Little Skellig – are a World Heritage Site. They rise sharply from the Atlantic Ocean about twelve kilometers west of Ireland's Ivereagh Peninsula. The larger crag, Skellig Michael, rises 700 feet over the waves, a sharp upward arrowhead pointing straight to heaven.

Located at the western edge of the European landmass, Skellig Michael was the chosen destination for a small group of ascetic monks who withdrew to this remote and inaccessible place sometime between the sixth and eighth centuries, seeking a life closer to God. They founded a monastery on this tall, precipitous crag, building with their hands a series of small dry-stone igloos – six beehive cells and two oratories. There they gave rise to one of the most extreme examples of Christian monasticism ever known, spending their days with nothing but prayer, salt air, sea birds, a vast sky, and ungodly weather.

At some point they brought a cow out there, grazing it in a small, natural saddle of meadow below the rocky summits. Picture a tiny, wave-tossed dory loaded with monks and a cow, getting a poor unhappy beast off the pitching deck and onto the rocks. It's astonishing.

Little Skellig is one of Ireland's most important breeding sites for seabirds, hosting on its ledges huge swarms of huge Gannets with six-foot wingspans, along with bright Puffins, Arctic Terns, Fulmars, Cormorants, and diverse gulls.

Gasping at the huge clouds of birds as we make our approach, I ask the fisherman, "Do they stay here all year?" He looks at me like I'm stupid and huffs, "No man – come winter, they're out to sea!"

Looking around and seeing nothing but watery horizon, I think, aren't we already out to sea? Ever since then, the thought of a warm-blooded creature surviving months of wintry gales on the open North Atlantic has made me shiver. But then, the huge Skellig rookeries are only breeding and nesting sites; to find an abundance of food, it's out to sea they go.

Hiking up the hundreds of steps to the top of Skellig Michael, I'm amazed at the human capacity to live at these extremes. Here on a

bright clear August day I can barely imagine
how this remoteness must close in during long
months of winter cold and fog. Days and nights
of wind-driven rain, with no barrier against the
onslaught but these piles of cold rock and an
abiding faith that this is what God is. A fearsome
God and surely at times a brilliantly beautiful
God, but for most of the hours of most of the
days, strung like endless rosary beads, a fierce
unrelenting God with little mercy for madness
brought on by cold relentless wind, crashing
waves, and crying seabirds.

How long might I have survived it, I wonder.
Maybe just long enough to go stark-staring
mad. How many, I wonder, just shrugged at a
certain point and jumped off?

Despite these thoughts, I can also feel a deep
spiritual pull in this place. Not a sense of
nearness to God so much as intimacy with
what we like to call nature. Looking out from
that vantage yields a clear measure of just how
small we are and just how powerful the forces
arrayed around us. Just how large our tiny world
is when we sit at its edges and look out upon
it. Early humans used just this sort of vantage

– an elevated ledge overlooking expanses of savanna or sea – to sit, stare, think, and grow mind. To see what's coming and what has passed and might return. To feel the eternal pull of the cycles. To feel immensely small but fully significant in its presence.

For those who have floated up to the Skelligs, climbed those hundreds of steps and looked out over the edge, the notion of hitchhiking to heaven has real appeal. It's a pilgrim moment of understanding that others have come and looked and staked deep belief, making their way here, and onward from here.

Hitch Haikoo

A poem sequence written whilst hitchhiking
my ancestors' Emerald Isle in the year 2000

Carry-on: camera,
notebook, recorder,
water, a few of my
goodly longings

•

"My mother's brother's
daughter's daughter"
on the shuttle at O'Hare

•

Single Irish-American mother with
three teenaged wild girls and a
cerebral-palsy son whom they all
love and guard. Him wailing in his
wheelchair at the check-in counter –
the girls embracing in tears.

•

"Bees on a sunny day suck honey from fuchsia" –
Aer Lingus seat covers
imprinted, James Joyce's fist

•

Make sure tray tables
are clipped up

•

Eyes closed in flight, imagining
Skellig Michael – by the skin
of our teeth we hang on through
"the precarious passage from
classical to medieval"

•

Interminable wait
for the jetway
"learner driver" and,
of course, for the
bleeding baggage

•

Against the rain
a dark-suited fellow
holds the Irish Times
against his head

•

Figures on roads

•

Dublin is swift, as
constant as its
graceful rain

•

Francis Bacon at Hugh Lane:
a figure on a sofa enclosed in a frame.
Snarling popes, mangled torsos,
enclosures that don't quite contain –
the verticals – moment's gravity
in depravity.

•

Good and evil,
ugly beauty,
side-by

Here, everyone
smokes everywhere

•

Hand-writ sign behind bar at Kennedy's Pub:
> Star News unless sport
> TV off at 6
> Lights dimmed at 9

•

Dublin rain comes fast,
pedestrians scatter, all
wet – water now,
laughter later

Laughing River Liffey
guides the people along
its swirling course

hang my shirt
out the hotel window
to dry

make mockery of sorrow
and hay while the
sun shines

•

Baggage Tragedy

Bereft but for
the clothes I wear
freed from all

not quite naked,
but traveling light

•

Where in the world
is it? Plain black
canvas duffel, all

my stuff sitting some-
where but, not here

•

Lively cryptic production
of DeLillo's *Valparaiso* at
Crypt Arts Centre, Dublin Castle –
thrilling, the more so by virtue of
a near fistfight in the audience
between an old man (WILL YOU
KINDLY SHUT UP!) and this kid
who's laughing at every line.

Come intermission the kid is
swarmed by elders, one of whom
says to him TAKE YOUR FOOKIN'
ECSTASY AT THE CLUBS, NOT AT
THE THEATER! The crowd debates
in hushed circles – who's to say
what's funny? – earnest conversation
'til the show (the Show!) resumes.

•

Yet to find a
bad cup of coffee
in Dublin – even
without the whiskey.

•

Sad, earnest faces of
elders don't quite
trust the good times.

•

End of day
en café
Saint Stephen's
Green

•

On Aer Lingus'
dime after fourth
day of baggage loss –

New Trousers!
Clean socks!
Underwear!
No longer sensing
the drift of my
own stink, as
Felipe might say.

•

American kids
assertive
Irish kids reserved
sans the weight of
forced irony,
though brands
are creeping in

Irish bear a
sense of clear
measure, more
fundamental human
beings so it seems
to me, the passing
stranger

•

It's raining in Dublin,
raining in me –
a fine soaking loneliness.

Fine, as I came here
for this – wanting to be
with my fellow strangers
and finally, alone.

At a window overlooking
Trinity College courtyard
and the campanile,
passing umbrellas shielding
people – one by one –
in drizzling privacy.

Eager to be wet but
cloaked from that in
soaking self-same solitude.

Here's hoping it
rains all night.

•

Heading to the North
I'm advised several times
in conversation, don't
hitchhike there – if
you're lucky you'll only
be beaten and robbed.

•

Up at eight, scalding shower,
breakfast at Take-5 on
Lincoln Place, quick stop at
Alexander Hotel to see Susanne
and let her know my baggage
tragedy continues and where I'll
be and when I'll be back.
Check out of Trinity room and
sidle over the Liffey on a smashing
sun-soaked morning past the Customs
House to the Bhusara – the bus station.

Unlike most American bus depots,
this is reasonable with lots of rucksack kids,
older Irish tweeds and foreigners galore.
Goood to see yeh!

People queue up, not compulsively like in
Ohio but with a certain cheerful restiveness —
chirping birds on a wire.

G'bye Dhublinn.
I'll be back.

•

Bandit Country

Stout clouds,
golden-gray

reflect the soul
of a hillock.

•

They don't take well
to the heat but it's
summer and there is
none. So, they're fine.

•

Heading for
the North,
this smiling
driver takes
only cross-border
passengers

•

Irish bikers
take daring chances
never seen in the
States – and on the
wrong sides of road

•

British fort below Newry in
South Armagh the first sign of it –
thick military antenna, armored
video cameras, forbidden ground
shielded from view. But watching,
listening.

Approaching Belfast from south,
a road-sign chiller: H.M.P. Maze
("Long Kesh")

The much-bombed Europa,
the Grand Opera House –
an arrival like any other
but with differences.

•

In the hotel bar two
women screeching
in anger, their men
holding them back –
uncivil war restrained
by tattooed arms
grasping for peace.

•

Cracking the Belfast egg
gently – the so-called
Golden Mile first. I ask
a cabbie if he'll take me
there and he grasps my
arm saying You're there!
It's here! and provides
expansive directions for
finding the best of it, with
lots of pointing and waving,
the earnest heartfelt
conversations seen down
in the Republic. So I walk Great
Victoria Street, Bedford Street
and Donegal, stopping to peek
in the front door of the Grand
Opera House where matron Marie
invites me in to take a look at the
ceiling, over-the-top Victoriana
with a curious smallness to it all.
In 1991 a 450kg truck bomb blew
a hole in it, then another in '93 –
but Marie shrugs, you just go on.
So now, again resplendent, the
Opera House stands in proud defiance
of its troubles.

John Jordan,
black cab driver —
God bless him.
Takes me on a
sobering ride thru
West Belfast, the
Shankill Road, the
Falls Road to Milltown
Cemetery and Bobby
Sands' grave, where I
kneel for a moment
and gaze at the crushed
white limestone the
Irish use to bed their
graves. John Jordan was
here for the grenade
attack after the Gibraltar
killings — Michael Stone,
now a hero on the
Shankill, attacked an IRA
funeral, killing how many?
He ran up that hill from
that highway right there.
I just dove for cover like
everyone else.

•

Sacred ground, nothing
sacred but the struggle
from either side.

•

Volume of everything five notches too high
here, bar bands blasting covers, elevator muzak
roars, Brit army choppers thumping overhead
sans cease. The drunks are way way loud – men
and women. Effect is somewhat numbing.

Only the Falls Road (the Catholic side) is quiet.
Quietly skittish.

•

Awakened by a woman's screams GET OFF
ME! attempted rape below my hotel window,
on the main drag on a late-but-busy night. As
I watch the RUCs are throwing the drunken
perp into a van, while the woman staggers off,
still screaming down Great Victoria Street. The
soldiers barely notice that she's gone.

•

Big moon rising in the east.
Big but not full, praise Jaysus.

•

The sons and daughters of Belfast
drink it all up. Their thirst is eternal,
and the resulting raptures are fierce
and free of conventional wisdom.
You hear bottles smashing on the street
all night. On Saturday morning on the
Falls Road I watch little girls playing with
shards of green glass.

•

Peace more than absence of war, and here war
barely absent. The Divis Flats loom over the
lower Falls Road with the roof and top floors
serving now as a British army base – men are
flown in, men are flown out, their feet never
touch the ground. They evacuate their trash.
Choppers from the rooftop, reminiscent of
Saigon 1975 only the Brits ain't leaving quite
yet – holding on to the top four floors of the

last remaining slum tower of the empire with a stiff upper bleeding lip.

The West Belfast "Peace Line" more a war zone – these people are scarred, Irish Permanent, and while there's a strong push for a lasting peace all compromise comes hard with little forgiven and nothing forgotten. This place is a typical post-colonial shambles, one can hardly escape feeling that blood will flow again.

•

There are times you miss out, just not thinking. I'd brought along a tape recorder and had it with me in West Belfast but the batteries were low so I left it in the room. And then John Jordan takes me down the Shankill Road and along the so-called Peace Line to the Falls Road and Milltown Cemetery, burial place for scores of IRA dead. In near thirty years of ferrying ABC news crews though the Troubles, John has brushed up against his maker and the devil, his easy talk bearing the weight of his own eyes upon it. I wish I had his every word. Say hi to Peter Jennings for me, he says as we grasp hands goodbye.

Later, I walk down the Shankill with my camera through a checkpoint of armored cars and the Royal Ulster Constabulary soldiers to watch the parade. Santa's not in this one.

Johnny Mad Dog Adair is out of Long Kesh, free on the streets with scores of other hard Loyalist men released under the Good Friday Accords. Masked paramilitaries are marching to a drumbeat in ancient British battle regalia, the Red Hand of Ulster. I try to hang invisibly, not wanting to be seen as a lone outsider, standing out in the crowd. I'm advised to Move on! in two wary chats with men not marching but watching. This isn't for you here.

I take some photos then walk past a phalanx of new recruits, dozens of tough young teenaged boys assigned to stand in formation on the Shankill Road as a buffer from any attack coming down past the checkpoint. Kids itching for a fight with community blessings. As I float by I watch them watching me and decide then and there this isn't for me here.

As I walk back toward the checkpoint, Mad Dog bounds up onto the stage amid a crackling volley of celebratory gunfire. Walk don't run, they're not shooting at you – I walk past the checkpoint and see the soldiers crouched down behind the armor. We exchange quick looks and I keep walking.

Later, I'm back at the Europa when another rattling blast of automatic weapons comes – the parade attacked by a factional mob, a pub shot up, six men hit, two dead. Brit choppers hover low in the sky all night.

•

GUN FURY
ROCKS
SHANKILL

blast the
morning
papers.

•

Northern Irish dark humor:
at a construction site
a stenciled sign reads
POST NO BILLS
the last word scrawled over with
BOMBS

Graffitied
on a
Shankill
wall:

SANTA
SEMTEX
PLEASE

The grinning skull

•

Belfast City Centre shuts down at 6pm
on Saturday – and once it does, it feels
hostile, though vacant. Best to come
mid-week and make your departure
before the blood drains out of the place.

•

They have nothing
in their whole
imperial arsenal
can break the spirit
of one Irishman
doesn't want to be
broke

Bobby Sands
5 May 1981

•

Courage swallows
fear, starving for the sake

The Road Out

Portadown decked
with Union Jacks,
all the storefronts
steel shuttered on
Sunday afternoon
(except for the
locksmith shop)

A3 south
to Armagh –
sheep asleep,
litter scarce,
neat small
stucco homes,
roundabouts

fat cows lowing
slow going

•

This landscape has the character
of open water – big slow swells
trimmed by hedgerows – oceans
of pasture

Road sign says ELDERLY PEOPLE
and another GIVE WAY

Through sun showers past
Armagh planetarium –

When the bus stops all the
pretty girls get off in a gaggle,
and the quiet woman with
the pot of lilies

•

When blondes go gray
they light up the world,
silver in gold

•

Your smiling face

•

In Armagh another
fortified outpost,
the cameras,
the Red Hand,
watching. Orange
flags all over.

Security raised
to a low art –
unscalable fences,
skirts on police vans
to keep firebombs
from below.
Meanwhile cows
loll in meadows
cut by hedgerows
and dry-stone walls.

What kills
us kills
them too.

•

At Cavan the bus biddies stream in,
bless themselves and have their tea
and biscuits in their seats – birds of
a feather on a slow glide to Galway,
chirping brightly all the while

•

Walking Galway, looking for the light

•

Easy to float
in the Galway rain

looking for someone
name of Sharon

we met on the
Belfast bus

she got on at Cavan
we got off at Eyre Square
walked together to
the Great Southern

leaving me, her
smile dazzling
much as the rain
now dazzles
cobbled streets
misting windows
giving float to
longings way,
way back

•

'Things seem empty
on vacation if the
labors have not been
physical'

so I look for her
at the Quays
finding instead this
hot smoky bar crush
and a young girl
crying drunk
in the gutter

Things seem empty

But near offshore
wild islands jut from
the North Atlantic

and people clung
to those rocks –
their labors physical,
they huddled
in a firm gale

•

Just
hunky
dory

On the Thumb

First ride with
Maive Joyce from
Burna to Spiddal
restores my faith
in hitch-hiking
karma

After I'd hiked
all the way from
Galway to Burna
half of it backwards
thumb out
hat on, hat off
shades on, shades off
trying all the combinations
to look harmless
getting discouraged
note (I thought): it
ain't the sixties
na moore

But then, brave Maive
former hitcher herself
the sun breaks thru
Earth tilts

we talk the whole way
about Ireland and America

Then in Spiddal, my
spirits renewed and calves
no longer cramping, these
two lovely French kids
Julien and Celine
give me a ride and a smoke
all the way to the ferry slip
at blessed Rossaveal, where
we sit for beans and chips
with malt vinegar, weak coffee –
small comforts are best

Celine's lively brown eyes,
the way she touches her lip
to think of the English for me

She loves it here
very much

-

Cutlery are NOT like
medicine they are NOT
to be taken after meals
The Management

-

Aran Isle Inishmor
more limestone
running out to sea
from the Burren,
surfacing here
for newcomers to
gather stones into
long low lines,
build soil from sand,
shit and seaweed,
cross-hatch the
island into geometries
of definitive fences,
low stone walls
everywhere, to grow
potatos and parsnips

"Sheets of gray-blue
rock with flowers
and grasses bursting
through the cracks"

ancient pre-Christian
settlements, the remnants

and now, tourists and
other seekers, this being
August – the craic is good

•

Things no longer
seem empty, the labors
have been physical

The world is full
Ta an domain lan

•

Bus Eirann

A horse chasing
a horse chasing
a bird –

cows, no silos, green

•

Two young American guys,
cousins I think, named
Irish though they're not

Their puerile snorts viz
the red-headed girls: do
the rug match the curtains?

•

A horse with a bent
stick in its mouth –
a horse prancing her
colt around a field –
crows watching

•

In Ballyngarry
a keg line-up
crowds a sidewalk

•

On Aran Isle the
ground bled rock

•

Gangly
reaching
pines

smaller
scrubs

cedar
lines

•

River Laune
at Killorglin

•

Long day on the road –
Galway to Limerick
Limerick to Killarney
Killarney to Cahersiveen

Now famished in heaven
O'Driscoll's Town House
('that won't be long,' she says)
for a Guinness, smoked
mackerel ('mind the bones')
and Irish lamb stew –
green beans, boiled carrots
and turnips, a bowl of
skin-on boiled potatoes –
a massive wholesome meal,
with buttered brown bread

Best one so
far by far

•

The Irish say "brilliant"
when they mean "okay"
or "that's fine" or

brilliant, say, like sun
on breezy water or
long morning and
evening arcs of light
as slender fingers on
the green, dazzling
a limestone wall or
granite erratic from
the last ice age

Making change at the deli
counter, the young girl says it
to end our brief transaction –
"brilliant"

You walk away
with the sense
you've been shined

•

Next day Skelligs are X'd
the boats all booked
couldn't land the last
two days for rough seas
now a backlog so, no go

All the way down
to Cahersiveen
for nought but

I do meet leprechaun
Patrick Joseph Foley
on the bridge over
the River Ferta

On Patrick's worn lapel
is pinned an image of the
Virgin Mary and, above it,
a Heineken button

Now

He wants me to
bring him a wife
from America

Now

She must have the cash
She must do the laundry
Come back next year
and bring her here

Now

He brings me into his
home, a tiny cramped
flat with a coal burner
and many, many clocks,
crucifixes, the pope,
a bag of Polish coal
in the bathtub

Now

Patrick Joseph Foley
lives now lives in the
present his blue eyes
rheumy but flashing
with big desires
in a small place

He waits and watches
the bridge, never been
to Skellig he says but,

Now

•

Up early to hitch-haikoo
to Cork, to Cobh, where
my people took their
departure, never coming
back. They stepped from
the rock to the bobbing
ship and made off for
America

but no

word of an opening on a boat
bound for the Skelligs – I drop
my bags at the hostel and make a
dash to the dock where the two-
legged fish are jumping into a boat,
handing over punts for privilege

To Skelligs we chug on the sturdy
Ken Brencent across what feels like
open sea on a brilliant morning

Sea birds glide above small soft
waves in this hard wet place –
hard, to be sure, when a day is
not like this, when the seas really
roll. Today – full sun, not a cloud,
flat water, our boat charging across
to the refuge, the UNESCO World
Heritage Site known as Skellig Michael

We spot the rocks, bolt upright spires
from the same rock beds made Ireland
but this an absolute verge out here

all exposed and touching God if God is
ocean, atmosphere and birds – scores of
gannet and kittiwake and storm petrel,

whole clouds of them haul it out here to
rook on the lesser of the Skelligs. They
winter at sea, if you can believe it,
and nest here from March til August

Guillemot, razorbills, puffin – they come
and go to this last place, where Coptic monks
came in the sixth century to meet God in
the solitudes

For centuries quiet men lived here on
this saddle of rock and laid six hundred dry-
stone steps, 150 meters up from the waves

Fishermen from the peninsula rowed them
out in their working boats and put them onto
the rocks, once delivering off a small pitching
currach a live cow to pasture in the tiny green
saddle up above and provide milk

With loose chunks of stone they stacked
igloo stone oratories and beehive cells to
live in and a small courtyard with weathered
cross, once sharp and newly-tooled, now salted
and wind-worn in a lee-side nook

Just enough space in the monastery for men
to brush by quietly and sit in prayer through
wicked storms, watching – closest to God, to
facts of fierce wind and ideas of radiance

•

Hitch-haikoo from
Portmagee back to
Cahersiveen with a
woman, two sons
and a dog in a tiny
Ford with a bad clutch.
One kid has a pot of
bread stuffing on his lap,
and a fork – the dog a
red Cocker Spaniel but
resembles Irish Setter,
long elegant eyelashes
and a shock of blonde
on its sturdy red head.

•

I see Patrick Foley again
down by the bridge, he
shows me his birth

certificate (I'd asked his
age yesterday and he
didn't know, but

remembered to bring
me this) – 22 October 1922
making him 78 now

feeble but strong, he insists
I drink tea from his
blackened mug as we
eat sweet muffins from
his fridge

Coal in his bathtub,
muffins and milk in
the fridge, seven clocks
at every turn, all set to
the right time, give
or take

Patrick Joseph Foley
Bridge Road
Cahersiveen
County Kerry
Ireland

send cards and photos

"she must have the cash"

•

Later the Skelligs overwhelming,
a strong spiritual residue

Imagine spending just one night there
alone on that rock, in one of those hives

Make another pilgrimage for a sit
when the circus ain't in town

•

600 steps
more or less
bring you up
to a quiet place
where monks
tread lightly and
stack rocks

closer to God
to the mists
and the birds
and all else

•

Herbert Mitchell from Tulsa Oklahoma
back at the hostel – we go for a pint
he's seventy-five and biking through

•

Next morning at dawn up and off
to the library which is also the bus
station where this complex intelligent
face appears – as I come to know her
between there and Dublin, she is Anna
Muntada, art historian from Barcelona,
traveling in a loose orbit with friends.
She learns English. She hunts old books for
her research. She makes page geometries and
looks for how we organize space in recording
ourselves and consciousness.

On a crowded train then a comfortable one
to Dublin we talk all day about everything,
all we know and what we don't yet know.
Lively deep-brown eyes flare above a smile
to light the way.

•

Anna's Story

So these two little sisters she says
are playing always playing in their
minds always asking questions so

their father tires of their tireless
queries and says to them I'm a-gonna
take you to the Wise Man, he'll

answer all your squeaky questions and
maybe shut you up! So he takes them and
on the way older sister tells her younger,

We'll beat this guy. I have a little plan.
She holds a captured butterfly cupped
in her capable hands and as she shows

her sister she says – I'll ask the wise guy
whether our lovely butterfly is alive or
dead? And if he says dead, I'll open my

hands and let it fly! But if he says alive,
I'll crush it before I open my hands!
We'll not be bested by this old goat.

So they arrive and warm up the Wise Man
with simple questions, as little girls might.
Just as he seems to relax into his big

wisdom big sister, her eye twinkling,
pops the butterfly question. Her fingers
lace a perfect cup and she searches

wiseguy's eyes back and forth as he
holds his gaze motionless on her hands.
With a slow deep grin his eyes rise to

find hers and he speaks in a soft
voice – the answer to that question,
he says, is in your little heart.

•

As a friend once said of China: you
go there and after a week you want to
write a novel of it. Then after a month
you think a short story, and after three
months a paragraph. When you've been
there a year your pen is poised but you
see you've barely parted the veil, and can
write nothing that makes real sense of it.

•

All Our Fish Are Fried

Bless us,
o Lord,
and these
thy gifts,
which we
are about
to receive
from thy
bounty,
thru Christ
our Lord,
amen.

•

I have the upper floor of Beshoff's
early & all to myself – a fine window
table – the black table tops clean,
ashtrays shining before the rubble of
the lunch crowd soon to arrive.
Watching pedestrian clusters on
O'Connell Street below, bright buses
and waking faces of a Friday morn.

Recalling the dramatic oil paintings of the
Easter 1916 Rising in the General Post Office
– the shine on the head of Michael Collins

Fried plaice, chips & slaw, coffee

•

The Spaniards
and Irish seem
parts of the
same puzzle

Italians something
else again

So many faces
from all over

often in pairs
but also, alone

•

We lean together
in rapt conversation
all over town

•

Sturdy
staggering
faces
looking
lost

•

Kids
drinking
openly
on the
street

tall cans
of stout
and hard
cider

too short
to vote but

not too young
to drunk

•

Wind has
the river
rippling

•

Flower boxes
black taxis
a line of bottles

•

Mountains
tilt onto
the sea,
with sweet
fogs of peat
burning

•

Old men
in doorways

spitting
their luck

•

Kelly or Ceallaigh: strife!
 – second most common name
in Ireland after –
Murphy: sea warrior!

Dad a Kelly, Mom a Murphy

Minogue is a monk
Dubh Linn the dark pool with
Joyce's slanting hand on those
pages at the Chester Beatty

•

Sad to be leaving Dublin today
another week here might be good
but home and work beckon so
I go back to my life feeling more
Irish than ever. Mass yesterday at
Saint Andrews nails it – flood
of holy memory, mine and those of
ancestral souls, seeming to pour
forth as sacrament, the holy moment,
blood into wine into blood.

∙

Worn ruck-sack desire –
to have you and lose you
is how life makes way.

Journeys too soon over,
we go anyway.

∙

Anonymous Irish Folk Poem on the Wall
at U.S. Customs & Immigration,
Dublin Airport

> My grief on the ocean
> it is surely wide
> stretched between me
> and my dearest love
>
> I am left behind
> to make lament
> not expected for
> ever beyond the sea
>
> My sorrow I'm not
> with my fond fair man
> in the province of
> Munster or County Clare
>
> My grief I am not
> with my dearest love
> on board of a ship
> for America bound

•

Upon ancestors'
new soil, roads taken outward
bring us here, and home

•

Jerry Kelly has worked as a technical writer, truck driver, construction lead and laborer, and in renewable energy. He now teaches photovoltaic physics and PV system design at Kenyon College in Ohio.

Kelly is the author of Bushville, a baseball memoir issued by McFarland Publishers in 2000.

www.ingramcontent.com/pod-product-compliance
Lightning Source LLC
Chambersburg PA
CBHW020400080526
44584CB00014B/1109